True Crimes in Victorian Times: Murder in Pocock's Fields

JAMES TIERNEY

DEDICATION

For May and Jimmy.

CONTENTS

ACKNOWLEDGMENTS

With thanks to the National Library of Scotland for access to their extensive records.

1 CHAPTER ONE

On Tuesday 17 March 1840, Mrs Mary Thornton asked her daughter, Elizabeth, to deliver some writing paper to her neighbour, Mr John Templeman.

It was around 8:30am on a cold and frosty morning when Elizabeth knocked on the door of Templeman's little cottage in Pocock's Fields, but there was no reply from within.

Templeman normally slept in a bedroom at the rear of the cottage, so Elizabeth went to the bedroom window. The window was shut tight, as it usually was, and Elizabeth stood on her tiptoes and tried to peer over the small curtain inside, but was too short to do so. The tenacious Elizabeth then went to the sitting-room window, which lay open, and called out to Templeman, but she was greeted only by an eerie silence.

Elizabeth returned home and told her mother she had been unable to gain access to their neighbour's property. Slightly concerned, Mary Thornton retraced her daughter's steps, but her attempts to elicit a response from within the cottage also failed.

Mary moved to the rear of the cottage where, unlike Elizabeth, she could see over the bedroom curtain. The bed was empty, but Mary's eyes widened as they fixed upon the battered and beaten body of John Templeman. The body lay on the floor, about a yard from the bed, with the feet pointing towards the fireplace and the head towards the parlour door.

The shocked woman went to the sitting-room window and found it was open. In the four years she had known Templeman, Mary had never seen the sitting-room window open. It had previously been fastened with a little button, lying just below a broken section of the window that had previously been covered by thick paper. The paper was now missing. With the paper gone, it was possible for someone to have reached in through the gap and unfastened the window. The window, when opened, was big enough to allow entry to the parlour.

Frail septuagenarian John Templeman lived in a small compact little cottage built as part of a development on open land at Pocock's Fields, Islington.

Pocock's Fields were situated on the west side of Liverpool Road and lay about one mile from the Islington Turnpike. They formed part of the well-known White Conduit Fields and were bounded on the west by the road running past White Conduit House towards Holloway.

Mr Templeman's cottage was known as 'Lincoln Cottage', named after the county in which his family had formerly lived. The property had been built at the expense of Templeman's grandson and had a fine view of the neighbouring area. To the north-west lay Highgate Tunnel, Highgate Church and Caen Wood, the seat of Earl Mansfield. To the north-east, one could look upon the towers of Holloway Episcopal Chapel.

Templeman's neighbours were generally from the poorer classes, though he himself, having retired from his work as a damask weaver, had a steady income from a couple of properties he rented out.

Although not exactly an 'Ebenezer Scrooge', Templeman was known locally to live a frugal life, though he took great delight in giving the appearance of being a man of means and never tired of boasting to his neighbours of his property portfolio. Inevitably, word of his comparative wealth spread further afield.

On 16 March 1840, Templeman set off for Comer's Town, to collect the rent due from the two properties he owned there. He returned with £6 in silver safely tucked away in his pocket.

At about 5:45pm the same day, Mrs Mary Thornton, a neighbour who acted as his charwoman and ran errands for him, looked in on Templeman. The unfortunate trait of 'flashing the silver' meant Templeman could not resist showing off the money he had received in rent. Templeman put the silver into a little mahogany box, which he placed onto a table in the centre of the room.

Templeman was in the habit of retiring to bed at six o'clock at night, so, at about 5:55pm, Mrs Thornton bid him a good evening and returned to her own home. That was the last time she would see her neighbour alive.

Mary Thornton, her daughter Elizabeth and her son-in-law, Francis Capriani, lived in the cottage directly opposite John Templeman's. Three other cottages neighboured Templeman's, these were occupied by the Jarvis family, Mr and Mrs Downes and Mr & Mrs Mustow. All the cottages were surrounded by palings.

On discovering the dead body of her neighbour, the appropriate action required seems rather obvious, however, a traumatised Mary Thornton decided, rather than immediately summoning the police, she would await the return of her son-in-law, Francis Capriani, who would shortly be finishing his shift as a night-watchman at Sadler's Wells Theatre.

Sadler's Wells Theatre, in Islington, was originally opened in 1683 by Richard Sadler. The theatre's name was derived from a combination of Sadler's own name and a well from a monastic spring discovered on the land he had bought. Over the years, Sadler would make increasingly outlandish claims regarding the healing properties of the water from the well. The theatre thus gained fame as a unique house of entertainment and healing.

Over the years, as other wells were discovered and new theatres opened, Sadler's Wells Theatre went into a steady decline. By 1840, the audience was largely made up of a drunken and boorish clientele. The wealthier patrons from the City that were adventurous enough to venture into the suburbs for entertainment, were provided with escorts, arranged by the theatre's management, to ensure they could safely make their way back into Central London after darkness had descended.

On top of his job as a night-watchman, Francis Capriani supplemented his income by carrying out handy-work for Mr Templeman. On 16 March, Capriani had dug and tidied Templeman's garden and later that evening he had collected his reward of seven shillings. The money was made up of six shillings and two sixpenny pieces. Templeman had taken the coins to pay his handyman from the little mahogany box that stood on the table in the centre of the room.

Capriani had noticed the box contained half-crowns, shillings and sixpences.

It was 11am on 17 March before Capriani returned from his shift at Sadler's Wells, to be greeted by his, clearly upset and agitated, mother-in-law. Mary Thornton brought him up to speed with what she had seen at Templeman's cottage and, after taking in the scene for himself, Capriani decided on the next course of action.

One might assume this next move would be to inform the police, but no, instead Capriani decided he would set off to inform Mr Templeman's grandson, whom Capriani was aware worked close by, as a solicitor, in Mortimer Street, Cavendish Square.

Whilst Capriani was away on his quest to appraise Templeman's grandson of the situation, the local baker arrived at Templeman's cottage with the regular delivery of bread, only to be met by Mrs Thornton, who informed him there would be no reply at the cottage door that day.

Shortly afterwards, Capriani arrived back at the scene, with Templeman's grandson in tow. When he had taken in the horrific sight of his frail grandfather's blood-soaked body, young Templeman came to the obvious conclusion, that this was a matter for the police.

It was 11:30am when Police Constable William Kear of N Division, accompanied by two surgeons, Mr Roe and Mr Lord, first appeared at the crime scene.

Kear tried the front door but found it to be locked. The constable then entered the cottage through the sitting-room window and opened the door, to allow entry to the surgeons. The door had been locked from the inside and the key was still sitting firmly in the keyhole. The cottage had only one main door and there were two further doors inside, providing access to the two interior rooms. A wooden partition separated the two rooms.

The constable found the body of John Templeman, dressed only in a nightshirt, lying on the floor, adjacent to the bed. The victim was flat on his back, with his feet laid towards the fire-place and his head towards the window. The man's hands were bound in front of him with cord, one cord tied around his wrists and a smaller cord tied around the other restraint. A stocking had been placed over Mr Templeman's eyes and had been tied in a knot behind his head. Another stocking lay on the floor beside the body and both stockings were soaked in blood. Kear deduced the stocking covering the man's eyes had been taken from the floor where he lay, as there were bloodstains on both sides of it.

At that point, Sergeant Collins arrived on the scene. Collins began his own search of the property and noted the top two drawers in a chest-of-drawers had been prised open, presumably with a chisel. Inside the top drawer was an empty mahogany box, about ten inches long by six inches wide.

As Collins searched the furnishings, Edward Roe, one of the surgeons, was engaged in a more gruesome search. He picked up one of the victim's teeth from a blood-soaked pillow, one from a chair and another was discovered in a pool of blood on the floor.

Roe then examined the body of John Templeman. The hands and nails were blue, due to the pressure placed on them by the man's struggle against the cord that had been tied tightly around his wrists. There were several bruises on the victim's face and he had suffered a severe blow to his left temple, a cut to his nose and fractures on both sides of his lower jaw.

The surgeon observed four clean cuts on the back of the victim's head, one or two bruises on the breast bone and further bruising on the collar-bone. The man had suffered abrasions to his knees, no doubt caused when he had been struggling on the floor. There was blood on the floor, immediately under the deceased's head, about ten ounces worth. Roe considered the man's wounds would have been likely to have continued to bleed for some time after death. There was no contused wound on the left temple to cause the blood, and Roe believed a good deal of the blood would have come from the injuries to the jaw and the clean cuts on the back of the head.

Regarding possible murder weapons, Roe ventured the wound on the temple and the fractures to the jaw had most probably been inflicted by a blunt round instrument, similar to a policeman's staff, perhaps by a piece of wood. The wound on the nose was likely to have been from a kick, or something of that description, not inflicted by a sharp instrument. The wounds on the back of the head were inflicted by a very sharp instrument, possibly by a chisel.

Lying next to the body was a small piece of wood, about three inches long, that appeared to have splintered from a round stick. The wood was saturated with blood, in which strands of hair, similar in colour to that of the victim, were stuck fast.

Roe's initial thoughts were the man had been dead for five or six hours. The body was generally cold, but there was a little warmth around the heart. He considered the blow over the left temple would have been sufficient to have caused instant death.

Police suspicions were aroused by the length of time it had taken to report the crime and they immediately took Francis Capriani into custody. Capriani was, however, able to account for his whereabouts on the night of the murder and, when he was brought before the Magistrate the following day, 18 March, no evidence was produced against him. He was formally discharged with no stain on his character.

The investigation continued at pace and later the same day, three new suspects were placed at the Bar, before Mr Combe, at Hatton Garden Police Court. The new suspects were twenty-four-year-old Richard Gould, a sickly-looking man dressed in a shooting-jacket, twenty-five-year-old John Jarvis and his wife Mary Anne, who was cradling her eighteen-month-old son in her arms. The two male prisoners were handcuffed and the police ensured they were protected from the angry mob that spewed into the room, as word of the arrests for the brutal murder spread through the neighbourhood.

Combe began proceedings by asking if Mr and Mrs Jarvis were related in any way to the other prisoner, Gould. Inspector Miller, of N Division, replied they were not. Miller was then sworn in.

The Inspector stated that, after the Police Court examination of Francis Capriani, he had made further enquiries to trace the murderer of the deceased, John Templeman. Miller had been made aware known criminal Richard Gould had been discharged from his job as a potman at the Barnsbury Castle Public House in January and had since dropped off the radar.

After asking around the neighbourhood, Miller had received a tip that Gould was known to frequent a beer shop in York Place. The informant led the Inspector to a cottage in Pocock's Fields, adjacent to John Templeman's cottage, where he believed Gould had been residing.

Miller had knocked on the cottage door and asked the owner if he was aware of Gould's current whereabouts. He had been delighted to hear Gould was in the bedroom. Miller had crashed into the room and called out, 'Gould, I'm looking for you.' The startled suspect, who was in the bed with two children, replied, 'What for?' Recognising the policeman, Gould had demanded, 'Where's your warrant?'

'I wish to speak with you regarding the murder of Mr John Templeman,' the Inspector had said to Gould. 'Aye, give a dog a bad name and hang him,' Gould had replied. The Inspector had then searched his suspect and found nine shillings and sixpence in silver in his trouser pocket, seven Lucifer matches in his waistcoat pocket and a brand-new pair of laced shoes beside his bed. A subsequent search of the property would reveal a further £5 in cash and some clothing stained with blood. A velvet waistcoat, belonging to the suspect, was marked with blood and part of it was burnt.

'What connection have the prisoners Jarvis with the prisoner Gould?' Combe asked.

'Mrs Jarvis was known to have lived with Gould, and her cottage is but a short distance from that of the deceased,' Miller replied.

Mr Mallett, the Clerk of Court, then chipped in, asking Miller, 'On what grounds did you apprehend the man Jarvis?'

'In his lodgings, we found a bag containing a shirt that appeared to have been used to wipe bloody hands and, on searching the cottage, I found a cotton stocking and cloth cap belonging to Gould.'

The next witness to be sworn in was Mrs Mary Anne Allen, of Wilson's Cottage, Pocock's Fields. Mrs Allen was so overwhelmed by her court appearance, she testified from a chair that had been rushed out to stop her from keeling over.

When she had finally composed herself, Mrs Allen revealed Richard Gould had been a lodger of hers some twelve months earlier, until he had become resident potman at the King William the Fourth Public House. After several months, he had left that job and taken work at a local iron foundry. About four months ago, he had turned up at Mrs Allen's door in a distressed state, saying he would be willing to help her out in her business of selling potatoes if she would offer him lodgings. After he had found his feet again, Gould had gained employment as a potman at the Barnsbury Castle, Islington.

Allen continued her testimony, stating that, the previous Sunday, Gould had turned up at her cottage again and she had allowed him to stay on a night by night basis, sharing a bed with her two children. He would leave each morning at 9am, return in the late evening and be asleep by 10pm. He did not take his meals at the cottage.

At around 8am on Sunday 8 March, Mrs Jarvis had turned up at Allen's cottage, inquiring after Gould. On hearing he was still in bed, Mrs Jarvis had left without seeing him, though she had left two eggs and some bacon for him. She had called again at the cottage on the next two mornings and had left with Gould on each occasion.

'On Sunday 15 March,' Mrs Allen said, 'the prisoner got up at about 9am and said he was thinking about going to his cousin's over the water and did not want to go in his dirty neckerchief. I lent him one of my husband's neckerchiefs and he set off. He returned at about 1pm and said he was very ill. He claimed to have been drinking beer on an empty stomach and lay down until 6pm. When he rose, he gave me sixpence to buy something for tea. He informed me he had made £1 during the day.'

Mrs Allen went on. 'The next morning, Monday, Mrs Jarvis called again, but she did not go into his room. She called on him to get up and said she and her husband were about to have breakfast. He said he would come directly then he got up, got dressed and left. Gould stayed out that night and did not return until 1:30am on the moonlit Tuesday morning.'

'I had left the door unbolted for him and when I heard him coming in, I said, 'Richard, it is very early, it is morning.' That was all that passed between us before he went to bed, there was nothing peculiar in his manner. I got out of bed at 7:30am on Tuesday morning and when I went into the wash-house, I heard Gould pass through and enter the privy, closing the door behind him. Five or six minutes later, I saw him standing at the table, near the window, and he was doing something to his trousers. He then asked for a towel to wipe his face and after enquiring what time it was, he left the cottage.'

'Did you discover any blood marks on his clothing?' Combe asked.

'No,' Mrs Allen replied.

'Did any of the money recovered later by the police belong to you?'

'It did not, sir,'

In reply to further questions from Combe, Mrs Allen said, 'The stocking and cap that was found belonged to the prisoner, Gould. I saw the stocking, the one the Inspector has produced in Court, on Monday morning, with its fellow, by the side of Gould's bed. When he went out on the Monday morning, he had been wearing a pair of heavy nailed shoes. They were quite old, but still wearable and certainly too good to be thrown away.'

'On Tuesday morning, Gould left, as usual, wearing the heavy shoes, and after I had warned him I would not leave the door open for him if he did not come back at a respectable hour, he returned at 7:30pm. When he came in, I remarked to him, 'What a shocking thing, to have so horrid a murder committed so near to us.' Gould replied to me, 'I have heard about it, I heard it at The Rainbow.' I said to him, 'How come you have not heard of it before?' At that stage, my husband interrupted and the matter was dropped.'

Mrs Allen would have been glad she was seated, as her lengthy testimony continued. 'Gould said he was thirsty and gave my husband a shilling to fetch some beer. I asked him why he'd been back so late on the Monday night/Tuesday morning and he said he had been at The Rainbow. He claimed he had then gone to see his cousin and aunt, from whom he'd received some money, and he had given his old shoes to his cousin. When we resumed discussing the murder, Gould said there were many poor fellows who would rather be hung than transported. The subject of right and wrong came up and he said he did not believe in the bible. Gould then smoked his pipe, before retiring to bed.'

Mallett asked Mrs Allen if she was aware of anything missing from her cottage since Sunday last, to which she replied, 'Yes, a cheese knife.'

Combe then asked what Gould had been doing when the witness had seen him in the wash-house, had he been cleaning his trousers? Gould interjected, to declare, 'I was washing myself, it was 8:30.'

With that, Mrs Allen's evidence was concluded.

The next witness to be called was Police-Constable Seamans, of N Division.

Seamans stated, 'I apprehended the male prisoner, Jarvis, at 5am yesterday morning, in Pocock's Fields. When I saw him leaving his cottage, I asked him if he had heard about the murder. He replied, 'Yes, it is a shocking affair.' I asked what time he had got home at on Monday night last, and he said, 'At about 6pm.' I walked with Jarvis to the station-house and took him in. He said he was innocent, knew nothing of the murder and was willing to go anywhere to prove it. I searched him and found a handkerchief with a spot of blood on it and three shillings in cash. I also found a glazier's knife. Jarvis is a painter by trade.'

Next up was Police-Constable William Kear, who declared, 'I apprehended Mrs Jarvis at her cottage at 7am yesterday morning. I asked her if she knew a person named Gould. She replied, 'I know of no such person. I know of a man named Richard, who formerly lived at the Barnsbury Castle.' I asked when she had last seen him and she replied, 'On Sunday last.' I asked if she was sure that was the last time she had seen him, and she said, 'Oh, no. I met him in Liverpool Road at 8am on Monday morning.' I asked her whether she knew what became of him afterwards and she said she did not.'

Kear continued. 'I told her she should accompany me to the station-house. She said, 'I hope you will let my husband know.' I searched the cottage and, lying on a set of drawers, I found a chisel that corresponded with the marks on the window of Mr Templeman's cottage.'

The parade of police witnesses continued with the calling of Sergeant Richard Bradshaw, who said, 'On Tuesday evening, at about 6pm, I went to Jarvis's cottage and saw a large crowd had gathered. I heard Mrs Jarvis say to her husband, 'The old man is dead, he has been killed.' The husband appeared agitated and said, 'I know, I have heard of it.' I then heard Mrs Jarvis say, 'Go in and see him,' to which her husband replied, 'No, I feel ill, I am very sick.' I then watched them go into their cottage. I did not follow them or speak to them. I was dressed in uniform at the time.'

'So, they were aware you were a police officer?' Mallett asked.

'They were,' Bradshaw replied.

The policeman continued. 'This morning, at 7am, I accompanied Sergeant King to Mrs Allen's cottage. We conducted a search and found a stocking containing nineteen crown pieces, one half-crown and over four shillings in change. The stocking was tied up and concealed between the tiling and the rafters of the water-closet. It belonged to the prisoner, Gould.

We then went to Jarvis's cottage and, among the bedclothes, found a shirt with spots of blood on it and a blood-stained rag. Surgeons later said they believed the items had been recently used.'

Bradshaw went on. 'At 10am on Tuesday morning, at the station-house, I asked Gould, 'Is the shirt you are presently wearing the only one you own?' He replied, 'No, Mrs Jarvis washes for me.' I remarked upon the shirt that had been found with spots of blood on it and Gould said, 'It is not the first time I have had blood upon my clothes."

The police surgeon, Edward Roe, then provided evidence regarding his examination of Templeman's body.

At this stage, Combe asked the prisoners if they had anything they wished to say.

An ice-cool Gould replied, 'I think it best to wait until all the evidence has been gone into.'

John Jarvis stated, 'I can only say I knew nothing of the circumstances of Mr Templeman's death until I returned home at night.'

Mary Jarvis declared, 'There were only one or two persons outside the cottage when my husband returned home, not the large crowd the policeman claims to have seen.'

Combe said he would remand all three prisoners for further evidence, but stated he was of the view there was already sufficient evidence to bind them over to appear at the Central Criminal Court.

With that, the prisoners were led from the bar and taken off, through a crowd of curious onlookers, in a police van.

From the early hours of the morning of the resumption of the inquiry, crowds gathered outside Hatton Garden Police Court, hoping to catch a glimpse of the three people suspected of the murder of John Templeman. The respected members of the community jostled with those less respected, as they all tried to gain access to the body of the courtroom to witness day two of the Inquiry.

When the police van containing Richard Gould, John Jarvis and Mary Ann Jarvis arrived at its destination, crowds swarmed around it like flies around excrement and the policemen had to battle their way through the baying mob to deliver the prisoners before Mr Combe.

Combe had spent the morning at the scene of the murder, inspecting Templeman's cottage and the surrounding neighbourhood. Proceedings finally resumed at 1pm.

Gould exuded an air of calm and his youthful countenance betrayed no sign of anxiety as he was placed at the bar. John Jarvis, on the other hand, was a trembling, feverish, downcast mess of a man, though his attractive wife remained cool as she cradled her child in her arms.

Before proceedings continued, Inspector Miller had a quiet word with Combe and informed him the Coroner, Mr Whateley, had halted the Inquest into Mr Templeman's death. Whateley had informed the Inspector he required the attendance of the three prisoners on the adjournment day of the Inquiry before he would be able to conclude the Inquest.

This did not impress Combe in the slightest and he declared to the Inspector, 'I will grant no such request. I have nothing to do with the Coroner, nor he with me. The prisoners are appearing before me and I will investigate the matter and place them on remand from time to time until I have determined whether to commit them for trial. Should I decide to commit them for trial, whether that be on Saturday next, Monday next or any other day, I will be sending them directly to Newgate.'

Mr Greenwood, who was sitting on the bench, concurred with Combe and stated he could not see what the Coroner's Inquest had to do with the Magistrate.

Having calmed down somewhat, Combe said he presumed Whateley wanted to show the prisoners to the jury at the Inquest. He told Miller to inform the Coroner that if he wished to contact him, he should do so in writing and Combe would provide a written response. Miller said he would do as the Magistrate had asked.

When the Inquiry finally got underway, the gallery gasped as the first exhibits of the day were placed before the Magistrate, three of the murdered man's teeth and a piece of a stick covered in blood and human hair. Combe suggested it would be essential to the investigation to clear some of the blood from the wood, to determine what type of wood it actually was.

After Miller had produced the cord and string with which the deceased's hands had been tied, the first new witness of the day was sworn in.

Charles Allen began, 'I am a shoemaker and reside at Wilson's Cottage, Pocock's Fields. The prisoner, Richard Gould, slept at my place seven or eight nights past. He slept there, I believe, on Saturday night a week ago.'

'The prisoner was unemployed,' Allen continued, 'so, in consequence of his poverty, I never asked him for money. He sent me for some beer on Tuesday night last, after the murder, at about 7:40pm. He gave me a shilling to get some beer and something to eat. I went and got him half an ounce of tobacco, a rasher of bacon and a pot of beer.'

'On Monday morning, at 8:30am, Gould left the cottage. He was dressed in the same clothing he has on today. He had his old heavy shoes on, or half-ankle boots, which were well nailed. He returned home on Tuesday morning, between 2 and 3am. I was awake at the time but did not speak, however, my wife said, 'It is very late or very early,' to which he replied, 'It is very early.' From his manner, I should say he appeared sober. He then fastened the door and went to bed.'

'I saw him the following morning, at 8:30am, when he passed through the bedroom, before going into the wash-house. If he had thought properly, he could have gone into the garden to access the wash-house at any time of night without our knowledge. I cannot tell whether he went into the water-closet, I was having breakfast. He was in the back part of the cottage for about twenty-five minutes, then he passed back through our room and went out.'

'At 11am on Tuesday morning,' Allen said, 'I heard a person had been found dead. I went to the deceased's cottage and I saw Mrs Jarvis coming in the direction leading from White Conduit House. I saw the prisoner, Gould, at 8pm that night. I returned home and found him there, sitting in a chair near a table in the centre of the room. I sat down and a conversation about the murder ensued. He said, 'Do you suppose he has done it to himself?"

At this point, Gould leapt to his feet and called out, 'Allen, you are under oath, this statement is a gross falsehood.' Unperturbed, Allen continued his testimony. 'I said, 'Richard, it is highly unlikely he would have done it to himself, or his hands would not have been tied, nor his eyes covered.' He then went into the backyard and returned about ten minutes later, complaining of illness. I was at supper and he said he would like something to eat, then he asked if I would go out to get it. I said, 'Can't you fetch it yourself?' and he replied, 'No, I don't want to go out."

An increasingly animated Gould called to Mr Combe, 'May I ask him a question?' The Magistrate replied in the affirmative and Gould said, 'I want him to explain why I did not wish to go out.'

Allen responded. 'There was a warrant against him for an assault and he did not wish the neighbours to see him, but he did not tell me that at the time.' His saga then continued. 'Gould accounted for the money he had, by saying he'd been to Lambeth and Wapping to call upon his aunt, who had subsequently given him some money. I don't know where his aunt lives, I've never met her, but I believe she is very respectable. In the evening, I noticed he was wearing new shoes and he said his cousin had given them to him. He'd had his old shoes for about eight months, I'd made them for him and they were perfectly serviceable.'

'Gould is a good scholar,' Allen continued, 'and he knew the Scriptures well. He frequently spoke about them with my wife, but he was very contrary and always differed with her on the subject.'

'Had he any conversation, relative to his religious beliefs, on the Tuesday night?' Mr Mallett asked.

'He said if the Scriptures be just and true and the Messianic laws right, he had broken them all.'

'My suspicions had been awakened towards the prisoner on Tuesday afternoon,' Allen said, 'when I saw Mrs Jarvis on the pathway near the deceased's cottage, on her way home. I had a suspicion there was an improper intimacy between Gould and Mrs Jarvis. I had a good reason for my suspicions, based on what I had seen between them, and I believe if one did the murder, the other would be aware of it.'

Mallett then asked, 'So, when you questioned the prisoner on the Tuesday night, were you fishing for information?'

'Yes, I was trying to elicit what I could from him through my suspicions,' Allen replied

'Did the prisoner say anything else that struck you?'

'Yes, he said he would rather be hung than transported.'

The suspicions of Charles Allen continued to be laid out. 'Gould said he had been at the Rainbow Public House the night before, until about midnight. This he said to me on Tuesday morning. When I asked him why he didn't get back to the house until 3am, he said he had been talking to someone whom he had met. I said to him the murder was a very serious affair and it was strange anyone would commit such a horrid crime for such a trifling sum of money, hardly worth the snuff of a candle. The prisoner then went to bed and I immediately fastened the door to his room.'

'Why did you fasten the door?' Mallett asked.

'Because I never intended he should come out again,' Allen replied.

'Did he hear you fasten the door?'

'He must have.'

'I intended giving information to the police regarding my suspicions the following morning and hoped to have him taken into custody,' Allen continued, 'but Inspector Miller came to the cottage that night and took him. On Tuesday morning, I noticed a cheese knife was missing from the mantle-shelf. I had used it on Monday.'

Gould again jumped to his feet and asked, 'Haven't you often used knives in the garden and left them there?'

'Yes, but not that knife,' Allen replied.

Gould was not for letting the matter rest. 'Were the children not in the habit of using knives in the garden and leaving them there?'

'Yes.'

'Anyone could have entered the garden, it was quite open,' Gould stated emphatically.

'All of the gardens and wells have been searched and examined by the police,' Allen said, 'but no knife or other weapon has been found. The knife to which I refer was the sharpest one I had.'

Gould, who seemed intent on taking over the inquiry, asked, 'Did your wife not go out with baked potatoes on the Monday night?'

'Yes, but she did not take the knife,' Allen replied, concluding his testimony.

The next witness to be called was John Frinabley, the landlord of the Rainbow Public House, Liverpool Road, Islington.

'I recall the prisoner, Gould, being in the bar on Monday night, 16 March,' Frinabley began. 'He was there all evening and left at about 11:40pm. In the early part of the evening, he had been playing skittles. During the latter part of the evening, he moved to the tap-room. He drank nothing but beer that day and appeared sober. He returned to the bar the following day, at about 8am, and was in the tap-room until 7pm, though he may have absented himself during that time, as I only saw him at intervals.'

Next up was Mary Elizabeth King, who had been drinking in the Rainbow on 16 March. 'I saw the prisoner in the Rainbow at about 11:45pm. He was wearing the same coat he has on now and had something in his coat pocket. It was something about a foot long and tied up at the end. It seemed to have a handle. I made a remark upon it to my husband the following morning, after I'd heard about the murder. I thought of Gould before I knew anyone had been taken into custody.'

Robert King, Mary's husband, was then deposed and he corroborated the statement his wife had provided.

The next witness was John Ellis, a painter, who described having met Gould and Mrs Jarvis on Tuesday 17 March. After he had told them of the murder, he had heard Mrs Jarvis say to Gould, 'You had better not go home.' The couple had not, in Ellis's opinion, seemed surprised at hearing of the murder.

Before the day's proceedings were ended, Mr Combe asked the prisoners if they had anything they wished to say. Gould declined to speak, John Jarvis said nothing had been raised about him over the course of the day and Mrs Jarvis said, 'I'd heard nothing of the murder until John Ellis told me of it.'

Mrs Jarvis then asked the court to re-examine the shirt found at her cottage, claiming it belonged to her husband and not Gould. This prompted Gould to break his silence and ask the court to also re-examine his waistcoat, claiming the surgeons were wrong and the marks on the waistcoat had been there for a considerable time.

Having found his voice again, Gould asked if he might have a copy of all the depositions. Combe said he may, then the Magistrate brought a long day of Court business to a close.

2 CHAPTER TWO

As attention focused on the Inquiry at the Hatton Garden Police Court, a small drama played out at the cottage of the murdered man.

The policeman guarding the cottage, where the body of John Templeman still lay, was surprised to be confronted by two extremely agitated women demanding entry to the property. One of the women, a lady aged between sixty and seventy years old, claimed to be Templeman's wife.

Having been previously informed Templeman had been a widower for several years, the policeman politely asked the women to calm down and informed them he could not allow them access to the property. He was placed on the back foot when the woman claiming to be Templeman's wife produced a copy of her marriage certificate, showing the couple had been married at Greenwich Church on 20 December 1833.

After inspecting the document, the constable apologised and allowed the women access to the cottage. Unprepared for the sight awaiting her, when she set eyes on her husband's savagely beaten body, Mrs Templeman slumped to the floor. After attending to the distressed woman, the policeman obtained a statement from her.

Mrs Templeman revealed the murdered man had been her third husband and said the couple had been separated for the past three years. She claimed the separation had been occasioned by jealousy and she had received no maintenance from Templeman.

The woman's first husband had been a Mr Cutler, proprietor, for upwards of nineteen years, of the Angel Inn, Islington. Following Cutler's death, she had then married a Mr Hinckley, an excise officer. Following the breakup of that marriage, she had married John Templeman.

Mrs Templeman informed the constable she had only become aware of the murder by reading of it in the daily newspaper. She then stated her husband was a native of Edinburgh and had been a damask weaver by trade. After moving to the cottage in Islington, he had purchased a machine for weaving bed-sacking.

Elsewhere, Inspector Miller was organising an intensive search of the area to locate the murder weapon. Door-to-door enquiries were followed by extensive searches of the gardens and the numerous wells in the area, but nothing to help the case was found.

The police were not entirely clear what kind of instrument of death they were looking for. The cuts and severe bruising on the head had given rise to a suspicion a hatchet may have been used, but the discovery of the piece of stick, matted with blood and hair, indicated a heavy piece of wood had delivered the fatal blows.

Miller was anxious to ascertain whether anyone had seen Templeman in possession of a stick or piece of wood corresponding with the splintered piece found at the scene of the murder. He harboured a strong suspicion the item Mrs King had claimed to have seen in Gould's pocket in the Rainbow Public House may have been the murder weapon.

Locating the cheese-knife that had disappeared from the cottage of Mr and Mrs Allen on the Monday morning was also proving to be difficult.

With the lack of material evidence proving a problem, Miller was also intent on finding out more about the relationship between Gould, Mrs Jarvis and Mr Jarvis. The information gathered by the Inspector appeared to indicate John Jarvis, known to the locals as a good man and hardworking painter, was unaware of the shenanigans taking place behind his back between his wife and Gould.

Suspicion regarding Mrs Jarvis's involvement in the crime was strengthening. She had known on the Monday night that Templeman had collected his rents and this, taken together with her relationship with Gould and the fact a bloody shirt belonging to him had been found in her cottage, led Miller to believe she had communicated Templeman's circumstances to Gould and had been involved in the planning of the robbery.

It had been noted that in the Police Court, Mrs Jarvis always sat next to Gould and away from her husband. The police believed there was a slow-burning resentment building within John Jarvis, as details of his wife's affair with Gould was laid bare in public.

Further information regarding the background of Richard Gould was beginning to emerge. He had garnered a reputation as a violent young man and had been in custody on charges of assault on numerous occasions. In June 1839, he had been brought before the Hatton Garden Magistrates on a charge of violent assault upon a publican in Islington, whom he had tried to strangle.

In January 1840, Walter Couch, a pot-boy at the King William the Fourth Public House, where Gould was the resident potman, applied for a warrant to be issued against Gould on the grounds of assault. When police arrived to serve the warrant, they found Gould had absconded with £4 of the pub's takings. He had subsequently dropped off the radar, until his apprehension for the murder of John Templeman.

The Inquiry into the murder of John Templeman resumed on Saturday 21 March 1840.

Crowds had gathered from early morning at the rear of Hatton Garden Police Court, to await the arrival of the police van as it delivered the three prisoners. The public gaze focussed on each individual prisoner, as they were hustled into the Court.

The attractive Mrs Jarvis cradled her equally attractive child in her arms and somehow seemed to rise above the chaos surrounding her as she strode serenely through the Courthouse door. Gould looked less assured than he had during the previous days of the Inquiry and his eyes darted around frantically as he appeared to search for a friendly face in the mob. Mr Jarvis looked as downcast as ever. He ignored his wife, but inside the Court, he took his child from her and kissed and embraced the child fondly. Gould and Mrs Jarvis exchanged knowing glances and wry smiles passed between them as they maintained silence while being transferred to the holding cells.

The trial had become the 'best show in town' and the gentry jostled with the lower classes to gain entry to the courtroom. Fearing the lower hall would not have sufficient capacity to contain the crowds, Mr

Combe ordered the larger hall on the first floor to be prepared and the Inquiry continued in that room.

At 1:30pm, the full bench of Magistrates finally took their seats.

The day's proceedings began with Elizabeth and Mary Thornton recounting the harrowing tale of how they had come to discover the body of their neighbour. Mary then told how Mrs Jarvis had been an occasional visitor at Templeman's cottage but had quarrelled over a sum of money, the balance of a loan the old man had believed was due to him. Mrs Thornton said she had not recently seen either Mr or Mrs Jarvis at Templeman's cottage but had seen Gould there, serving the old man with beer.

Templeman had been known to talk about his property, but Mrs Thornton had never heard him speak of having money in the Bank of England. He had, however, told her he collected around £4 per week in rent.

Mrs Thornton had last seen Mrs Jarvis on the previous Tuesday and had noted she was remarkably composed and untroubled. Thornton concluded her testimony by saying she had absolutely no knowledge of any undue intimacy between Gould and Mrs Jarvis and had never heard anyone mention it.

Combe felt obliged to chide Mrs Thornton for not notifying the police immediately after she had discovered the body. Mrs Thornton said she believed she had acted prudently and properly by informing the murdered man's grandson. She did, however, say that when such a circumstance occurred again, she would take care to follow the suggestion of the magistrate. This prompted Combe to remark, 'Why woman, you talk about these horrid things as if they were an everyday occurrence.'

Francis Capriani was the next witness to be called and he told the court he had seen Mrs Jarvis at the murdered man's cottage on the previous Monday afternoon. Capriani had been working in Templeman's garden at the time and he had seen the woman talking at the cottage door, but had no knowledge of what was being discussed. Capriani then stated he had no knowledge of any illicit relationship between Gould and Mrs Jarvis.

Next up was Henry Knight, a potman at the Duchess of Kent Public House, Lower Road, Islington. Knight stated he had seen Gould on Tuesday evening, the 13th, at the pub. Gould had asked for a half pint of beer and had thrown down a penny, claiming it was all the money he had. Knight had poured him a pint of beer but had not taken any money for it.

The Clerk of Court then said to Knight, 'You say this was on Tuesday the 13th?'

'Yes,' the witness replied.

'This cannot be right, there was no such day. Tuesday was not the 13th, Friday was the 13th.'

'Oh, then, sir, it was on Tuesday week.'

Gould was not amused by the Clerk of Court's intervention. 'That is not evidence sir, you are bound to take down what he says and not to instruct him as to what evidence he should give.'

The Clerk of Court decided to ignore Gould's interruption and Knight's evidence continued. Knight claimed Gould had told him he had been over at the Borough Public House, where he had met another unemployed man who was going to meet him again the following morning, in the Duchess of Kent. Neither man had subsequently turned up. Gould had also said to Knight that if he was made aware of any potential job opportunities, he could contact him at the home of Mrs Jarvis, where he was now staying.

This triggered Gould once again and he rose to exclaim, 'Take care what you say, remember you are under oath! I never mentioned Mrs Jarvis.'

The Clerk of Court stepped in to placate Gould. 'Please don't be impatient, your time for putting questions will come soon enough.'

The interruptions appeared to unsettle Knight and he seemed to freeze on the spot. 'Do not be deterred from speaking the whole truth,' the Clerk of Court said to Knight, 'you should not conceal anything you know, in consequence of the prisoner's observations.'

Knight finally pulled himself together and continued his testimony. 'There was nothing the prisoner said to me that would have indicated an improper intimacy existed between him and Mrs Jarvis and I have not heard anything from anyone on the subject. I had heard from Mrs Allen, with whom he was lodging, that she thought Gould was having 'a rum time of it', but I took that to be because he was not coming home at a seemly hour.'

'During a conversation with Gould,' Knight continued, 'he told me he knew of an old man who had £25 hidden in his cottage and he then said he had seen a further £50 note in the man's possession. Gould then said to me, rather brazenly, the old man would have been as well making a gift of the money to him, as he intended to get it anyway.'

'I asked Gould where the old gentleman lived, but he replied vaguely, 'No matter, it is not far off.' He then added, rather ominously, a poor fellow must do something when he has got no money. I took this to mean Gould intended to commit robbery.'

Following Knight's rather damning testimony, the next witness to be sworn in was John Richard Jobson.

'I live at 11 Dorset Street, Spitalfields,' Jobson said, 'and I have known the prisoner, Gould, for some years. On Friday, the 13th, at about 8pm, I found Gould standing in the passageway of my house as I was coming downstairs. I asked him what he wanted and he said he would like to speak to Jem Rogers, a day labourer who also stayed at the house.'

'I asked Gould what he wanted with Jem,' Jobson continued, 'and he said he wanted to speak to Jem about obtaining a 'screw'. I understood by a 'screw' he meant a pick-lock. I advised him Jem was not in, but if he went over to the public-house directly opposite, he would be sure to find Jem there very soon. Gould then told me he could not go to the public-house, as he had no money.'

'Gould then said to me he may also require Jem to get him a 'darkey', as he intended to 'serve an old gentleman out' and it might be handy. By 'darkey', I understood Gould to mean a dark lantern and by 'serving out', I took that to mean he planned to rob someone. I said to him, 'You'd better not do that, for if you do and get caught, you'll be sure to be transported.' He said he would take his chances and added he intended to serve out the old gentleman on the following day.'

Jobson's testimony continued. 'When I saw, on the Wednesday evening, the account of the murder at Islington, I said to a man who was in the tap-room with me, 'Good God, I could pick out the murderer from among ten thousand people.' I did not go to the police immediately, because, before doing so, I wished to see the account of the proceedings at the Inquest. When I saw the account of the Inquest, I went to the police at the Spitalfields station-house and told them what I knew. I also informed them Gould was a deserter from the army and that I had sheltered him for some eight days after his desertion. I then told them the man's real name was Arthur Nicholson.'

The prisoners were asked by Combe if they had any questions they wished to put to the witness. Gould said he had none at present, whilst Mr and Mrs Jarvis said as no evidence had been produced against them, there was nothing they needed to ask. Mr Jarvis complained about being returned to custody, given there had, to date, been absolutely no evidence presented against him, adding he also knew none could be.

Combe quietened the gallery before bringing proceedings to a halt for the day, though not before Inspector Miller had teased the crowd by stating a lot more important information would be produced when matters resumed on Tuesday. All three prisoners were remanded until then.

Pocock's Fields had suddenly become a major London tourist attraction, as the public and the newspaper reporters descended upon the little community like a plague of locusts. Many of the more curious ghouls attempted to gain access to the cottage of John Templeman and a twenty-four-hour police guard was put in place.

The newspapers depicted Pocock's Fields as being a locality akin to Nova Scotia Gardens in Bethnal Green, an area made notorious by the London Burkers, a group of body snatchers who modelled their activities on Edinburgh's Burke and Hare, in the early eighteen-thirties. This comparison was harsh, to say the least.

On Saturday 21 March 1840, John Templeman's body was placed in a neat coffin studded with double rows of black nails and covered with black cloth. On the lid was a plate, bearing the inscription, 'Mr John Templeman, died March 16, 1840: aged 72 years'.

Over at the New Prison, Clerkenwell, it transpired Richard Gould was spending the night sleeping in the same bed in which the infamous murderer James Greenacre had reposed, prior to his committal to Newgate Prison, where he was subsequently hanged. Greenacre had been convicted of the murder of Hannah Brown, whose body he had cut up and spread around the Edgware Road area of London in 1836. Greenacre and his lover, Sarah Gale, stayed firmly rooted in the London public's conscience, thanks to them featuring in an early display in Madame Tussauds Chamber of Horrors, which opened in London in 1836.

The press was hungry for information about Gould and a letter he had sent to the proprietor of the King William the Fourth Public House, Mr Bartlett, was leaked to the newspapers. The letter had resulted from an incident at the pub on 24 January, which had led to Thomas Crouch, a potboy at the King William, applying, at Hatton Garden Police Court, for a warrant against Gould for assault.

The warrant was granted by the sitting Magistrate, Mr Greenwood, and was placed in the hands of Mr Chicherley, an officer of the Court, to be served. Before the warrant could be served, Gould absconded with £2 of the pub's takings. What he left in exchange was the following letter:-

'Dear Sir,

You will, no doubt, be surprised when you receive this note, but as you thought it proper to give me a week's notice to quit, I have thought it proper, under existing circumstances, to leave tonight. It would be very foolish of me to get into trouble for the sake of a week's work, for I have been given to understand a warrant would be served on me in the morning.

I shall take this opportunity of putting you in possession of the accounts, as I intend to go into the country for a few months. If there is any difference between us, I will settle it on my return. There are three weeks wages due to me as of tonight, and I think, with the accounts I have sent you, it will make us about straight. There was 1s 5d left the last time I settled the beer.

I have no more to say at present but remain your humble servant.

Richard Gould'

On receiving the letter, Bartlett immediately informed the police Gould had absconded. He also provided them with a full description to assist them in tracking the man down.

Bartlett informed the press he was now convinced that if the police had shown proper diligence, Gould, who had been widely known to still be lurking around the area, might, long ago, have been apprehended on the charge of embezzlement and thus the murder of Mr Templeman may have been prevented.

On 23 March 1840, the Coroner, Mr Whateley, and a jury of householders that had been empanelled, assembled at the Barnsbury Castle Public House, York Place, Islington, to continue the Inquest they had been holding into the death of John Templeman. The crowds that had previously gathered at the Inquiry now switched their attention to the Inquest.

The first witness to be called was Inspector James Miller, who stated, 'I have three persons in custody on the charge of murdering the deceased. One is named Richard Gould, who is also known as Arthur Nicholson. The others are John Jarvis and his wife, Mary Ann Jarvis. These persons have been under examination at Hatton Garden Police Court, before Mr Combe.'

'Many witnesses have been examined in relation to the murder,' Miller continued, 'but, to date, no person has yet been committed for trial for the murder of Mr John Templeman. At the termination of the examination on Saturday, the prisoners were remanded until tomorrow, then they were taken to the New Prison.'

'Without requiring you to speak of the guilt or innocence of the parties in custody, do you believe they could afford any information in respect of the murder?' the Coroner asked.

'Yes, I believe one or more could afford important information,' Miller replied.

'Do you recollect the first sitting of the Inquest at this house on Wednesday evening?'

'Yes.'

'Did I ask you to deliver a message on that occasion to Mr Combe?'

'Yes, you did.'

'Did you deliver the message?'

'Yes, I did, on Thursday morning.'

'Did you state my message openly in the office?'

'Yes, I did.'

'Please be so kind as to repeat the message,' the Coroner requested.

'I presented your compliments and requested the prisoners might be produced here during the adjourned day,' Miller replied.

'What was the Magistrate's answer?'

'Mr Combe asked me to offer you his compliments and to tell you he intended to remand the prisoners from time to time until he had sufficient evidence to commit them.'

Clearly burning with resentment, the Coroner then asked Miller if the reports of Mr Combe's comments reported in the morning newspapers were accurate. 'Not exactly,' Miller mumbled.

The increasingly irate Whateley then vented his anger. 'This needs to be sorted. Mr Combe has virtually refused the presence of the prisoners at this Inquest and this is the third time Hatton Garden Magistrates have done this, in cases where parties have suffered the heinous crime of murder. Having heard, under oath, from Inspector Miller, that either one or more of the parties in custody would be able to afford the jury important information relative to the death of Mr Templeman, I intend to send a warrant to the keeper of the New Prison, directing him to send, or cause to be sent, the accused parties, so they might be present to hear what occurs at this Inquest.'

As the veins in Whateley's face and neck protruded further, he continued his rant. 'In the event of a refusal on the part of the prison keeper to comply with the terms of this warrant, then the question would arise as to whether he was guilty of a gross contempt of the Court and whether he rendered himself liable to such punishment as it was in the power of the Court to award.'

'In the meantime,' the exasperated Coroner stated, 'we shall continue with the evidence that has no direct reference to the parties accused. If, however, on the return of the messenger, it is found these parties are not permitted to come before the Inquest, then I shall suggest to the jury the propriety of our adjourning to the prison. If we cannot get the persons in custody to come to the Inquest, then I see no reason in the world why we cannot take the Inquest to them.

Whateley was not yet ready to move forward though and the tirade went on. 'It is utterly repugnant I am obliged to take these steps, but unless I do so, the ancient court of The Coroner's Inquest, one of the bulwarks of justice and liberty, is in danger of having its utility entirely destroyed.'

Was it now time to move on with the Inquest, certainly not. The bitter words continued to pour from the Coroner's lips. 'Supposing a collision should take place between the police, the soldiers and the people. What if the Magistrates themselves had been instrumental in causing such a collision and they possessed the power to keep in jail whoever they pleased? Would this not entirely frustrate the ends of justice?'

Whateley then moved on to provide a brief history lesson. 'The Office of the Coroner is a much older institution than that of Police Magistrates and ought, therefore, to be more respected. Such a thing as a Justice of the Peace was never heard of until the reign of Edward the Third, whilst the Coroner's Court had been in existence for hundreds of years before, affording its protection to the people.'

The historical background having been laid out, it was time to get back to the present problem. 'You have heard there are parties in custody who have been charged with the crime of the murder of the unfortunate man upon whose body we are now holding this inquest. No less than four examinations have been entered into before the Magistrates, at every one of which the accused parties have been in attendance, and yet, after such a full examination, you, the jury, are expected to go through this entire Inquest without the presence of any one of these parties.'

'If this is justice,' Whateley continued, 'then I do not know what justice is. What I do know is this is not the kind of justice I will submit to, so long as I hold the high and important office to which I have been appointed. The Coroner's Inquest, in a judicial sense, is one of the bulwarks of English justice. What is more important to the administration of the law, than that the fifteen gentlemen empanelled as a jury in so grave a case as the present, should have before them the best evidence that could be afforded?'

As an aura of self-importance encompassed the room, Whateley stayed on theme. 'What is more important than that a jury of neighbours should sit at the spot, or near it, where their fellow creature if it has been murdered, was murdered? What is more important than that A, B or C should be present to hear the allegations upon which citizens, perhaps neighbours, should decide they were guilty of an offence that entitled them to the disgrace of being tried before the bar of their country, so they might be able to offer some observation, in mitigation, if they thought proper?'

A line between the Inquiry before the Magistrate and the Inquest before the Coroner was 'drawn in the sand', as Whateley moved on with his relentless rant. 'I trust the jury is not tired. I am sorry to enter into this conflict with authority, but I am determined to maintain the rights and privileges of this Court, inviolate. The time when this conflict of authority should be decided has now arrived and I sincerely trust it will not terminate in restricting the utility of this Court.'

'Supposing the Magistrates make out the committal of the prisoners on the charge of wilful murder,' Whateley went on, 'still, the grand jury has the power to ignore the bill. If, however, a verdict of wilful murder is returned against any parties by this jury, then they must be tried. This is a very important fact and it shows the superiority of this tribunal over the Police Court.'

Finally grinding towards the conclusion of his speech, the Coroner stated, 'The course pursued to date would leave the impression a Coroner's Inquisition is a mere matter of form. If that were the case, it would be brought into ill-odour and disrepute and the sooner it was abolished the better. I, however, feel duty bound to furnish you with the best evidence I can and I, therefore, intend to dispatch a warrant to

Mr Kilsby, the governor of the New Prison, directing him to send the accused parties before me and this Court.'

Mr Bell, the Coroner's clerk, then read out the warrant, before Whateley asked Inspector Miller by what means the prisoners were conveyed to and from Hatton Garden and under whose charge they were at such a time. Miller replied that the prisoners were under the charge of the police and were conveyed in a large covered van, though he did not think the van could be made available to bring them to the Inquest.

The Coroner then turned to the jury. 'This, gentlemen of the jury, will be your verdict. I wish to have the assent or dissent of every one of you as to whether you deem it advisable and proper you should have the persons accused of this murder before you.' To a man, the jury assented to the propriety of the prisoners being produced.

Whateley directed the clerk to complete the warrant, then he passed it to the summoning officer to execute. Finally moving on, the Coroner asked Inspector Miller's opinion of the best witness to call, whose evidence would not directly implicate the accused parties. Miller suggested Mr Roe, the surgeon who'd carried out the post-mortem examination on the deceased.

Edward Roe, surgeon, of Brown's Buildings, Highbury Square, was duly examined. He repeated the evidence he had given at Hatton Garden Police Court, regarding the position and condition of the body when he had first seen it. Roe then informed the Inquest that, since then, he had had carried out a full post-mortem examination.

'The lower jaw was much fractured on both sides,' Roe said, 'with an irregular wound perforating the cheek, down to the fracture on the left side. There existed several contused wounds on the lower jaw and the upper lip. The inner surfaces of the lips were lacerated, probably by being forced in against the teeth, several of which had been knocked out. A slight and rugged puncture was found in the upper jaw, corresponding with the lower one. It is my opinion this had been inflicted by some small blunt instrument. There were also two or three similar punctures on the external surface of the lower lip.'

Roe went on. 'A wound extended from the right side to the tip of the nose, obliquely crossing to the left, completely dividing the septum and terminating at the left nostril. On the right side, this wound continued down in a straight direction to the commencement of the upper lip. There was a bruise on each nostril, one above the bridge of the nose and another in the inner corner of the right eye. A very extensive bruise was found on the right side of the face, over the articulation of the jaw, which extended above and behind the ear. There was also a lacerated wound on the left temple.'

The graphic description of the horrific injuries sustained by John Templeman continued. 'There were fourteen cuts at the back part of the head, three of which divided the periosteum or membrane. The remainder penetrated to the bone and had, evidently, been inflicted by a similar instrument. The hands and wrists below the cords by which they had been secured were of a livid appearance, with the nails blue and bruises on the knuckles. There was a bruise on the articulation of the right clavicle and one just below the articulation of the left. There were abrasions on both knees, in different parts of the legs and on the left arm and elbow.'

The dark tone of the surgeon's statement was unrelenting. 'On dividing the scalp, a considerable quantity of blood escaped from above and beneath the temporal fascia on the left side. The integuments, to the extent of about two-thirds of an inch in thickness, were gorged with blood. On removing the cranium, about an ounce of fluid blood escaped from an aperture which had been made therein.'

'On removing the dura mater,' Roe continued, 'the brain presented a generally congested appearance with, here and there, a considerable quantity of coagulated blood, particularly in the region of the left temple. On removing the brain, a fracture was observed, extending along the base of the skull, commencing in the left temple, passing in front of the temporal bone and terminating an inch behind the external process of the frontal bone, on the opposite side. The fractures of the skull were the cause of death.'

'Did you find any instrument corresponding with the wounds and blows inflicted?' the Coroner asked.

'No, I did not,' Roe replied, 'though it is my opinion the blow near the left ear was inflicted by a round stick, like a policeman's truncheon. The other bruises may have been inflicted by kicks from a person with heavy shoes.'

'Do you think, from appearance, the deceased offered much resistance?'

'I think he offered some. The cords around his wrist were not only tightly fastened, but the cord was tied between the wrists by a thinner piece, to make the restraints more secure.'

A member of the jury then asked, 'Do you think more than one person was involved and more than one weapon was used?'

'I believe there were two persons at least involved in the murder and a chisel may have inflicted the other wounds I have referred to,' Roe replied, bringing his testimony to an end.

Elizabeth and Mary Thornton then provided the Inquest with the same information they had provided to the Inquiry, regarding the discovery of Mr Templeman's body. The only new fact to emerge was that Mary had heard words pass between Gould and the victim during the period Gould had lived in the neighbourhood, while he was employed as a potman.

'Can I ask why you did not, on your discovery of the body, immediately inform the police?' a member of the jury asked.

'I did not immediately inform the police because Mr Templeman had specifically requested that, in the event of anything happening to him, my first course of action should be to notify his grandson,' Mary Thornton replied.

At this stage of the proceedings, Mr Tubbs, the police constable who'd been given the unenviable task of delivering Whateley's warrant to the governor of the New Prison, arrived back at the Inquest.

Tubbs explained he had seen Mr Kilsby, the governor, who had, apparently, been expecting him. On hearing the reason for Tubbs's visit, Kilsby had informed the constable that, with due respect to the Coroner and his Court, he did not have the power to accede to the warrant, as he held the committal of the Magistrates. Kilsby had offered to apply to Hatton Garden Police Court for the permission of the Magistrates to hand over the prisoners. Tubbs had then accompanied Mr Kilsby's clerk to Hatton Garden with the request, but, in the absence of Mr Combe, Mr Greenwood had refused to get involved in the dispute.

The Coroner then read to the jury the committal signed by Combe and directed to the governor of the New Prison, stating the prisoners should be kept in safe custody until the resumption of the inquiry. This set Whateley off again and he recounted to the jury the story of another murder Inquest, where two parties had been accused of murder. Combe had again been the Magistrate in charge of the Inquiry and, despite the Inquest being carried out in a room within forty yards of the prison where the two suspects were being held, the Coroner had been refused their presence at his Inquest.

'As you know, I had, before the sending of the warrant, proposed an adjournment to the New Prison,' Whateley said. 'On reflection, given that Mr Kilsby has evidently done all his duty will allow him to do in this matter, I feel it would be unfair to place him in an awkward position by proceeding there.'

'I do, however,' Whateley continued, 'believe it is essential to record who it is that is trying to destroy the power and utility of the Coroner's Court. With that in view, I believe it best to adjourn until we see what the Magistrates will do when their Inquiry resumes tomorrow. I ask you, could you, consistent with your consciences and the oath you have taken, consent to return a verdict of wilful murder against parties who had not been allowed to appear to offer a single word in mitigation?'

In reply to his own question, Whateley offered, 'I am sure you could not. The Magistrates are not the highest power in the land and I can tell you that, between now and our next meeting, I will seek the opinion of a superior authority, in the hope of laying this important and conflicting matter to rest.'

With that, the inquest was adjourned.

3 CHAPTER THREE

On 25 March 1840, the Inquiry into the murder of John Templeman resumed at the Hatton Garden Police Court.

The prisoners had been brought to the Court in the early hours of the morning to avoid the crowds. Gould, dressed in a waistcoat and sleeves and fustian trousers, showed little sign of stress as he walked through the backyard of the Court. John Jarvis was as dejected looking as he had been at each of his earlier appearances. He walked in silence until he arrived at the lock-up cells, where he then asked the jailer, Mr Waddington, to lock him in a separate cell, rather than in a shared cell with Gould.

Mrs Jarvis, cradling her child in her arms, gave the appearance of being above all that was happening and she walked into the building with a show of bravado. When she arrived at the cells, she offered Gould some bread she was carrying in her pocket but made no attempt to communicate with her husband.

The crowds that gathered to witness Mr Combe take his seat at 10am, comprised of the familiar mix of gentry and ordinary citizens from the neighbourhood.

Before matters could get underway, a messenger arrived with a letter from Lord Normanby, relating to the application from the Coroner, Mr Whateley, to have the prisoners appear at his Inquest. The letter requested Combe's attendance at the Home Office and the Magistrate immediately ordered a cabriolet and set off to meet Lord Normanby. It would be late afternoon before Combe returned to begin the day's proceedings, though he remained silent on the outcome of his meeting. He began by asking if there was any further evidence to be presented.

Inspector Miller told the Magistrate there was some new evidence to be introduced and he asked shoemaker Charles Allen, with whom Gould had resided, to come forward. Allen produced a block of wood and informed the Court that, some time ago, he had sawn it off from a larger block. The other piece of wood was now missing from his cottage.

'And what exactly is to be inferred from the production of this piece of wood,' Combe asked.

The Clerk of Court, Mr Mallett, responded, stating that at one of the earlier examinations, the police had produced a piece of oak covered with blood and human hair. This had been subsequently examined by a carpenter and the grain had been found to correspond exactly with the grain of the wood now produced by the witness, Allen. 'Coupled with the fact another piece of this wood has gone missing, the circumstances can be viewed as suspicious,' Mallett offered.

'Mr Allen, please describe the piece of wood that has gone missing from your cottage,' Combe said.

'The piece of wood I missed was about sixteen inches in length, three-quarters of an inch thick, three inches wide and was originally cut from the piece of wood I now produce. I was in the habit of using the wood as a seaming-board, in my occupation as a shoemaker,' Allen stated.

'Was the missing piece of wood heavy?' Mr Mallett asked.

'It was. It had four sharp edges and if it was used in a proper manner, it would be enough to knock down a horse,' Allen replied.

'Where was it normally kept?'

'I kept it in a cupboard at my cottage. I placed it on the central shelf to prevent apples falling off, it acted as a ledge. The cupboard door, as well as the cottage door, were always left open during the daytime.'

'When did you first notice this piece of wood had gone missing?'

'I first noticed two days after the murder. On the 19th, I saw the little piece of wood produced at this Office, the piece covered with blood and hair. I immediately suspected it might have been part of the same piece of wood I had placed in the cupboard. When I looked in the cupboard, I discovered the wood was missing.'

'Was the cupboard in your bedroom or your living room?'

'It was in my living-room.'

'Was the prisoner, Gould, in the habit of taking items from your cottage?'

'No, I never saw him touch any of my things, except my tools to nail his boots.'

'Have you yet found the cheese-knife that went missing from your cottage?'

'I have not,' Allen replied.

Mr Combe then turned to Gould and asked, 'Do you have any questions you wish to put to this witness?'

'No, I have no particular questions I want to ask him, but I should like a turner or Magistrate to try the grain of the piece of wood covered in blood and hair against the grain of the piece of wood produced today by Allen,' Gould replied.

One of the Magistrates, Mr McWilliams, examined the two pieces of wood but declared he could not say, with any confidence, whether the grain matched exactly. Combe suggested to Inspector Miller that he should arrange for the wood to be examined by a turner, or tradesman, who could offer the Court an expert opinion.

The next witness to be sworn in was Jem Rogers, who stated, 'I reside at 7 Dorset Street, Spitalfields. I have known the prisoner, Gould, for six years. I now know him by the name Arthur Nicholson, though, off and on, I have known him by the name of Richard or Dick. I knew him by the name of Richard before he enlisted as a soldier in the 11th Light Dragoons. He told me he enlisted under the name of Arthur Nicholson. Until two years ago, he always went by the name Richard.'

Arthur Nicholson had been a soldier in the 11th Light Dragoons, stationed in Canterbury. He had been confined to the guardroom on suspicion of stealing a watch, but had subsequently made his escape and was presently classed as a deserter.

Having completed his saga regarding the prisoner's name, Rogers moved on. 'The last time I saw him was last Friday week, at about 7:45pm, when I returned home with my brother-in-law and found him at my door. He said to me, 'Jem, you are just the chap I require to see.' I asked him why and he replied, 'I want you to lend me two 'screws' and a 'darkey'.' A 'darkey' is more commonly known as a dark lantern.'

'What did he mean by 'screws'?' Mr Mallett asked.

'He meant skeleton keys. I told him he might as well ask me for a £500 note as ask me for such things as these,' Rogers warily replied.

'May I remind you you're under oath to speak the whole truth and your own position in this matter is reliant upon you doing so,' Mallet declared.

'I said to him, 'Dick, we'll drop that subject now. I am sorry to see you as you are. I would treat you, but I have no money either.' I have not seen the prisoner since.'

'Why do you suppose the prisoner called upon you to ask for the 'screws' and dark lantern?'

'I suppose it was because he knew I had once kept an old iron shop and he thought I might keep such things in my house.'

'Have you any knowledge of ironwork?'

'I know how to clean a lock or anything of that nature.'

'How do you make your living now?'

'I left off my old trade of umbrella making and now work as a porter at the waterside,' Rogers replied.

Gould, who'd listened intently throughout the testimony provided by Jem Rogers, offered that it was merely the judgement of the witness that when he'd asked for 'screws' and a 'darkey', he had actually meant skeleton keys and a dark lantern. Mr Mallett put this to Rogers, who replied he had indeed only judged it to be so.

The next witness to be called was a pawnbroker, Mr Jackson of Manchester Road, Holloway, who produced a shovel he identified as having been pledged by Mrs Jarvis on 16 March. Jackson was followed by another pawnbroker, Mr Wallis, who produced a child's frock and a handkerchief pledged for £1 by Mrs Jarvis on 16 or 17 March.

Next up was a vital witness, at least as far as John Jarvis was concerned. William Pelham was sworn in and declared he was the foreman to Mr Jay, a builder from London Wall. Pelham informed the Court that John Jarvis had been employed by Jay, since 28 February last, as a painter. The last job he had worked on had been to paint some houses Jay was building next to the Eagle Tavern, City Road. Pelham stated he could account for the whereabouts of John Jarvis from 6am to 5:30pm on the days of 16 and 17 March. He completed his evidence by saying Jarvis was a hard-working man, whose conduct had been exemplary.

Painter Daniel Butler was called next. Butler revealed he was a fellow employee of Mr Jay and said he had worked with and taken his meals with Jarvis throughout the days of 16 and 17 March.

Mr Combe had heard all he needed to hear regarding John Jarvis. Addressing the prisoner directly, Combe declared, 'John Jarvis, after the evidence I have heard today, I am discharging you immediately. You may step away from the bar and have your liberty.'

There was a general nodding of approval to be seen around the gallery, as Jarvis stepped away from the two dejected prisoners left behind.

The Magistrate advised Jarvis he may leave as soon as he liked, but suggested the more privately he left, the better it might be. Jarvis thanked Mr Combe, then said, 'I hope I may take my child, sir.' This triggered an anguished response from Mary Jarvis, who cried out, 'No, you shall never have the child, it is my child and you shall never have it.'

Combe conceded he was not exactly aware of the arrangements at the prison, but offered that, as the child was two years of age and no longer suckling, he did not believe the prison was bound to receive it. It would, however, Combe declared, be for the sitting Magistrate and governor of the prison to decide.

Mary Jarvis was having none of it, calling out, 'John, you shall never have the child, it is mine and I will not part with it.'

Turning to Combe, Mrs Jarvis defiantly declared, 'I have seen a Magistrate who has told me it is my child and he has no right to it.'

Combe decided to let the matter rest for the moment. As John Jarvis was about to leave the courtroom, the Magistrate said, 'I suppose you'll go back to your work as normal?'

'I hope so, your worship,' Jarvis replied.

Mr Pelham, the building company's foreman, declared, 'We'll take him back directly, your worship, and give him work.'

A voice from the gallery then called out, 'If you don't, I will!'

A spontaneous burst of applause echoed around the room as a clearly overcome John Jarvis walked to freedom and into the welcoming arms of his friends and family. Such would be the feeling of sympathy for Jarvis, a collection to raise funds for him was swiftly organised by the local community.

In reply to the Magistrate asking him if he had anything he wished to say, Richard Gould replied, 'No, not here. I can give a full explanation of all the evidence, but what I have to say I shall say at my trial, where I will have access to professional advice.'

Mrs Jarvis stated she had nothing she wished to say.

The two remaining prisoners were then led to the holding cells by Waddington, the jailer. Before putting Mrs Jarvis into her cell, Waddington ordered her to hand over the child. A furious Mary Jarvis responded that she would never give up her child and she held on grimly. As Waddington removed the child from the arms of the distraught woman, she unleashed a volley of abuse. 'You bloody vagabond, you scoundrel, take your hands of my child, you bastard' Overcome by grief, Mary Jarvis then slumped to the ground in absolute despair.

Waddington carried away the wailing waif and delivered it into the waiting arms of John Jarvis. Cradling the child in his arms, Jarvis and his entourage headed back to his cottage in Pocock's Fields.

26 March saw the resumption of the Hatton Garden Inquiry and the calling of a new witness, John Bash, of William Street, Barnsbury Park, Islington.

Bash stated he had formerly owned 'Spring Cottage' in Pocock's Fields. He had known John Templeman for some time and, about seven months earlier, Templeman had offered to buy 'Spring Cottage' from him for £25. The cottage was located next to Mr and Mrs Allen's cottage, where Gould was living.

Templeman had offered to lay down a sovereign as a deposit on the cottage, but Bash had told him he would only accept a full up-front payment of £30.

'Did the deceased say he had more money?' Mr Mallett asked.

'No,' Bash replied.

'Where did this discussion about money take place?'

'At the gate of Mr Templeman's cottage.'

'I assume this proposed transaction was no secret around the neighbourhood?'

'I certainly did not treat the matter as secret.'

'Did he show you any money?'

'He did not.'

'Was the conversation held in the open air?' Mallett asked, despite this already having been already made clear.

'It was.'

'Do you know the woman Jarvis?'

'No,' Bash replied.

'Now, look at Gould. Do you know him?'

'Yes, he used to carry beer about around Pocock's Fields.'

As Mallett offered that this testimony tied in with what Gould had stated in public regarding knowing an old gentleman who has offered £25 to buy a cottage, Gould interrupted, stating, 'I was 100 miles away from London seven months ago, I was in Norwich at that time!'

'Do you mean to say you were in Norwich seven months ago?' Mr Combe asked.

'I guess it was seven months ago. If I was not there, I was at the William the Fourth, in Clerkenwell, but I was not near Barnsbury Park or Pocock's Fields.'

Sergeant Richard Bradshaw was the next witness to be called. Bradshaw revealed he had seen Mrs Jarvis returning to her cottage at around 3pm on the afternoon of Tuesday 17th March.

'Mrs Jarvis came from the direction of London,' Bradshaw said. 'She came past the deceased's cottage, where a large crowd had gathered. I did not see her speak to anyone, but after she had gone into her cottage, she came back out to cut wood for the fire and I asked her, 'Do you know anything about the old gentleman who has been murdered?' She said, 'Yes, it is a shocking thing. I saw him only last night and he told me he had been collecting his rents. He said he was very tired and was going to retire to bed early."

Bradshaw continued. 'I then said to Mrs Jarvis, 'The old man must have had money.' She said, 'Yes, this very cottage once belonged to him and he sold it for £15. I heard he is planning to buy it back again.' When she left the cottage at 4pm, I spoke to her again and she said, 'I knew nothing about the murder until I got home, for I had been visiting my sister to borrow a screw."

'That is not what I said,' Mary Jarvis called out, 'I said I went to my sister's house to get some screws.'

Mallet turned to Bradshaw and asked, 'Are you sure your account of what Mrs Jarvis said is accurate?'

'I am,' the policeman replied.

Mr Combe then asked Mary Jarvis if she had any questions she wished to put to the witness.

'No, Sir,' Jarvis replied.

Combe declared he would remand the prisoners until Tuesday when he would take further evidence.

'Are you telling me we are to be placed on remand yet again?' an irate Gould asked. Mary Jarvis looked like she was also about to raise an objection before Gould turned to her and said, 'Say nothing. Let the bastards do what they like.'

'Are we going back to New Prison?' Mary Jarvis whispered to Gould.

'Yes, they are a shower of bastards,' Gould quietly replied.

As he was being led from the bar, Gould declared, 'I wish to ask a question before I go.'

'Very well, stand forward and ask your question,' Combe said.

'I wish to ask if I can have my boots returned. Nothing has been said against them and at present, I am being asked to walk upon the ground with these worn boots on me.'

'You are not required to go outside,' Combe said.

'No, but I am obliged to walk upon cold stones,' Gould responded.

'You have got boots on.'

'Yes, but they are old and worn.'

'I suppose I might send for your aunt to ask if you can have the boots, it was from your aunt you got them, was it not?'

Losing the plot somewhat, Gould shouted, 'I am not obliged to answer idle questions from every idle person. I should have nothing else to do if I was to answer questions from everyone that might question me. If I want to buy a pair of boots, I am not required to tell everyone from where I bought them, let them find out themselves.'

Having drawn attention to the boots by his outburst, Gould was re-seated and Inspector Miller was called to give further evidence.

'I have discovered that a pair of boots that exactly correspond with those worn by the prisoner, Gould, were purchased at Mr Wilcox's, boot and shoemaker, of Tottenham Court Road, for half a sovereign. A person from the house of Mr Wilcox attended the time of the sale.'

Combe immediately directed that Wilcox, together with the person in his employment who had witnessed the sale of the boots in question, be sent for. A police officer was dispatched in a cabriolet to collect them, whilst the prisoners were returned to their cells.

Late afternoon saw Mr Wilcox and his servants arrive at the Inquest in a hackney-coach. The prisoners, who were locked in separate cells, were disturbed by their jailer, Waddington, as the newly arrived group were asked to identify them.

Gould, who sat, arms folded, at the furthest corner of his cell, refused to step forward as Waddington called, 'Gould, you are wanted.'

'I will not come,' the stubborn prisoner replied.

'But you must,' the jailer insisted.

'I will not move unless it is to go before the Magistrate.'

'Get yourself forward now, there are people here to identify you.'

'Oh, identify me, you would be as well making a puppet-show out of me,' Gould sneered.

The prisoner eventually ended the stand-off by stepping forward and fixing an icy stare on one member of the party who had disturbed him. This continued for an uncomfortable length of time, then Gould allowed his eyes to droop before he shuffled back to the rear of the cell.

Mrs Jarvis, who'd been watching through the bars of her cell, turned her back as soon as the group approached. Waddington was reluctant to go through the same rigmarole and was pleased to hear the group had already seen enough of Mrs Jarvis. As the group turned to leave, Gould called out to his fellow prisoner, 'They would be as well hiring a hawker's cart and driving us about in it to be identified. That fellow with the silver collar, does he not look queer?'

Gould and Jarvis were brought back before the Magistrate, as Inspector Miller produced a pair of half-ankle boots he had taken from Gould on Wednesday 18 March. The boots were marked with figures upon the soles.

John Walters, a fourteen-year-old in the employ of Mr Wilcox, was called as the next witness.

'The figures 8 and 92 on the soles of the boots are in my handwriting,' Walters declared.

'Are you sure?' Combe asked.

'Yes, I think so,' the boy replied.

'You mustn't think now, you must know,' Gould snarled.

'I believe the writing is mine, the figures refer to the size and cost price,' Walters said.

'Do you recognise the prisoner?' Combe asked.

'I am afraid I cannot swear to have seen him before.'

The Magistrate then turned to Gould and asked, 'Do you have any questions you wish to put to this witness?'

Gould haughtily replied, 'I shall ask him nothing. He has said absolutely nothing to affect me.'

Mr Wilcox was then called. 'I recollect it was on Tuesday 17 March, when I was in an upper apartment of my house, that I received a half a sovereign payment for a pair of boots which cost 7s 6d. I gave half a crown in change.'

'Can you recollect who brought you the half-sovereign?' Combe asked.

'I cannot, but my daughter, who is eleven years old, has since told me it was her. She is, however, unable to identify the prisoner as being the man who gave her the money.'

'Can you tell me, from their general appearance, for how long the boots before us today are likely to have been in use?'

'I should say they have been in use for a very short time, no more than a couple of hours.'

When asked if he wished to question the witness, Gould replied, 'I have nothing to say, I know nothing of this man.' When offered the same opportunity, Mrs Jarvis replied, 'No, I don't see how this concerns me at all.'

The prisoners were remanded in custody and the witnesses bound over to appear at the Central Criminal Court.

4 CHAPTER FOUR

At 10am on 26 March 1840, Mr Whateley, the Coroner for the western division of Middlesex, resumed his Inquest at the Barnsbury Castle Tavern.

Barely able to contain himself, Whateley began proceedings by addressing the jury, to bring them up to date with the latest position regarding his request for the attendance of the prisoners being held on suspicion of murder.

Firstly, Whateley declared he had been pleased to note the last proceedings of the Inquest had been accurately reported in the press. He stated this in the hope of contradicting an erroneous rumour that was spreading, namely, that he was hostile to the publication of the proceedings of Coroner's Courts.

'No man could be more anxious than I,' Whateley proclaimed, 'that the proceedings at these Inquests should be accurately detailed for the public and no man could be more indignant or annoyed when public matters are falsely reported for political purposes.'

Turning his attention to the matter of the production of the prisoners at the Inquest, Whateley revealed that, after the jury had adjourned on Tuesday, he had obtained an interview with the Marquis of Normanby, the Secretary of State for the Home Department. He had advised his Lordship of the circumstances of the case and had been advised that, since the matter was of the greatest importance, the noble Lord would consider the matter and provide a response the following day.

On the Wednesday, Whateley said, he had received a communication from his Lordship, part of which he would read to the jury. The relevant section read as follows:-

'Lord Normanby has informed the Magistrate of his opinion, which is the proper course of action to be adopted will be, not to commit the prisoners for trial until the Coroner has had the opportunity of bringing them before his jury.'

One might have thought this clear victory would have signalled the end of the matter, but no, it merely saw Whateley climb back onto his soapbox. 'Nothing could be more prejudicial to public justice than if parties who are accused in this Court are not allowed to be present when the accusations are made. I ask you, why should a Police Magistrate be hostile to a Coroner's Court and endeavour to throw every obstacle in the way of a Coroner's jury?'

As his question hung in the air, Whateley resumed his relentless rant. 'Magistrates have very important duties to discharge, but they are not more important than those of a Coroner. I am sure Mr Combe and other Magistrates must be aware of a case of murder that took place in Chelsea within the last year. A man going by the name Marchant was taken into custody on suspicion of having committed the murder. The man was brought before the Coroner; was present during the Inquest; was found guilty of wilful murder; was tried on the capital charge and was then executed. In that case, the accused did not appear before any Justice of the Peace, the only Magistrate he stood before was the Coroner.'

The Coroner seemed in no hurry to bring in the prisoners he'd been so determined to produce for the jury, preferring to continue his tirade against Police Magistrates. 'In times gone by, when a party was taken before a Magistrate on a charge of murder, it was customary for the Magistrate to postpone the examination of the prisoner until after the Coroner and his jury had sat on view of the body of the deceased, to ascertain whether it was necessary for him to go into the case at all.'

It was time for another history lesson from Whateley. 'I recall a case at Haynes, where a jury had been assembled to investigate the circumstances surrounding the death of a young man named Allsop. The Inquest occupied two whole days and during that entire period, the accused party was held in custody on the orders of the Magistrates of Uxbridge. Not once did the accused have the opportunity of hearing the evidence being brought against him. The jury found the accused guilty of wilful murder, a verdict with which I certainly did not concur. Nevertheless, the Magistrates had the prisoner brought before them and, after the examination of several witnesses, they committed him for trial upon the charge of manslaughter. This after a jury, who had been given no access to the prisoner, had already found him guilty of wilful murder.'

'I trust the decision by the Marquis of Normanby,' Whateley said, moving back to the matter in hand, 'will sufficiently admonish all Police Magistrates in London and all Justices of the Peace in the suburban districts of the metropolis, that Government will not sanction them in their obstruction of the proceedings of Coroner's Courts.'

Having laboured the point, Whateley finally neared the conclusion of his outrage. 'I trust I shall never again meet with such difficulties as I have encountered in this case. I also trust the superintendents, inspectors and police-constables will be directed by the Commissioners of the Metropolitan Police to give Coroners the earliest possible notice of cases where a human being has lost his life due to the malicious act of another human being. It would then be seen whether a Coroner could carry out public justice, by ordering a party to be taken into custody and committing him for trial, after a jury had returned a verdict of wilful murder or manslaughter.'

A collective sigh of relief spread around the room as Whateley, at last, turned his attention to the case before him. 'I believe one of the parties who had initially been apprehended on the charge of murder and had been placed on remand several times has been released without a stain on his character. I propose that to prevent any confusion regarding the evidence, we have the remaining male prisoner brought in first and examine those witnesses whose testimony only affects him. Afterwards, we will take the evidence of those witnesses whose testimony relates to the female prisoner.'

Richard Gould was brought into the court by Inspector Miller and was immediately directly addressed by the Coroner. 'As this examination is likely to take some time, perhaps you may wish to take notes on the evidence. If so, I will order that you be furnished with pens, ink and paper.'

Gould nonchalantly replied, 'No, I thank you for the offer, but I will recollect it all.'

'But it might assist your memory.'

An unwavering Gould responded, 'It does not matter.'

'If you desire to explain anything away, you will have an opportunity afforded to you after the examination of the witnesses. You will also be given the chance to make your own deposition,' Whateley advised.

'I can give a full explanation,' Gould claimed.

'You are not bound to say anything unless you wish to, as it may have the effect of incriminating you,' Whateley clarified.

Inspector Miller and Sergeant King were the first witnesses called and they repeated the evidence they had provided at the Inquiry. When King produced some bloodstained garments belonging to the prisoner, Gould stated, 'I cut my cheek some time ago, that's the way they came to be stained.'

Mary Allen was next up. When she spoke of Gould's return to his lodgings in the early hours of 17 March, Gould asked, 'Was it uncommon for me to come home late at night?'

'No.'

'Has he kept good hours since he has been unemployed?' Whateley asked.

'Yes, very good hours. I have only known him to be out very late when he has been working,' Mrs Allen replied.

As the clock struck 2pm, the Coroner adjourned for an hour to enable the jury to take some refreshment. During the break, Gould was furnished with a plate of ham and a pint of half-and-half beer. At least there were some benefits to being brought before the Coroner.

After everyone had been fed and refreshed, proceedings resumed with a statement from Charles Allen, who corroborated the evidence given by his wife. Allen added that he had suspected the prisoner of having been involved in the murder and said when Gould had gone to bed with the children, he had locked the door and said to his wife, 'I'll never let him out again.'

Gould interjected, asking, 'This man is giving quite a different version to the one he gave before the Magistrates. Will his evidence be compared?'

'It will,' Whateley replied, adding, 'you are also entitled to a copy of the depositions taken at this Court and those taken at the examination before the Bench of Magistrates. In the event of your being committed for trial, the Judges will compare the evidence.'

Mr Whateley asked for the next witness to be called and Sergeant Collins set off to collect Jem Rogers. To the policeman's surprise, Rogers was nowhere to be seen. When Collins reported the absence of the witness to the Coroner, a voice from the hall called out, 'He would be a fool if he did come forward.'

After a couple of further witnesses repeated the testimony they had given before the Magistrates, Whateley addressed the prisoner. 'In the absence of two or three witnesses whose testimony I consider to be important, it will not be possible to conclude the Inquest today. It is not compulsory for you to attend the next sitting of the Inquest, but if you wish to do so, please let me know and I will make the appropriate arrangements.'

Gould was removed from the room and replaced at the table by Mary Jarvis. After taking evidence from Francis Capriani, regarding his having seen Mrs Jarvis in conversation with the deceased on the eve of the murder, the Coroner heard from John Jarvis that his wife had been at home with him during the night of the murder.

The Coroner then asked Jarvis about a bloodstained bag found in his cottage during a police search. Jarvis said he did not know to whom the bag belonged and claimed to have never set eyes upon it until he'd seen it at the police station-house.

At this stage, Mary Jarvis spoke up to say her mother would be able to explain everything relating to the bag, but before any further witnesses could be called, the Coroner adjourned the Inquest for the day.

Proceedings resumed on Monday 30 March.

Ann Tomkins, the mother of Mary Jarvis, was the first witness to be called. 'I reside in Kilburn Lane, in the parish of Willesden,' she began. 'I was at my daughter's house on the day of the Queen's marriage, having the day before sent my eleven-year-old son round to her house with a commemorative leaf, enclosed in a course bag. The bag in question had been stained with oil colours at the workplace of Mr Harward, the floor-cloth manufacturer and paper-stainer.'

'The bag, which I can identify as the one produced in Court today,' Tomkins continued, 'was much soiled, as my son had previously been wearing it as an apron. The bag had not been returned to me after I'd sent it round to my daughter.'

'Will you swear the stains you see on the bag now, were present before you sent it to your daughter?' the coroner asked.

'Yes,' Tomkins replied.

Thomas Graham, a professor of chemistry at University College London, was the next witness to be called. 'On Saturday, I was given the bag produced in Court today, to subject the marks upon it to a chemical analysis, to ascertain whether they were, in fact, bloodstains. I carried out a full and proper examination and the result of my research proved, beyond a shadow of a doubt, the stains were not of blood. They were, in fact, produced by paint, in which iron had formed one of the ingredients. There were several gentlemen present during my examination, among whom was Dr Rees, and all concurred with my findings.'

The Coroner turned to address Mrs Jarvis. 'It has been stated by the man Ellis that he saw you, on the afternoon prior to the murder, conversing at the door of Mr Templeman's cottage. Is there anything you wish to say about that?'

'I merely went, with my child in my arms, to speak to him and then I went back to my own cottage.'

'Was it for any particular purpose you went or were you in the habit of speaking to him?'

'I frequently used to walk my child up to his ground and converse with him.'

'The jury may not wish to hear from you again,' Whateley said, 'and you are not bound to say anything unless you want to. Do you wish to make any statement?'

'No, Sir,' the woman meekly replied.

After confirming with Inspector Miller there was no further evidence to be presented relating to Mrs Jarvis at that time, Whateley ordered the woman to be removed and Richard Gould to be brought forward.

Gould, looking somewhat pale and drawn, took his place at the Coroner's table as Jem Rogers was called. Rogers repeated the evidence he had given before the Magistrates, leading to only one question from the Coroner. 'Did he say for what purpose he required a 'screw' and a 'darkey'?'

'No, he did not.'

'Do you have any questions you wish to ask this witness?' Whateley asked Gould, to which the prisoner responded, 'None whatever.'

Next up was Hannah Morgan. 'I live at 18 Skinner Street, Somer's Town. On the morning of 16 March, at about 11:30am, Mr Templeman visited me and borrowed £3. I had loaned him money in the past. I gave him the money in silver, made up of fourteen half-crowns and twenty-five shillings. Mr Templeman was suffering from a terrible cold at the time and could barely speak, but he told me he needed the money to make up a sum he required. One of the shillings I had in my possession had the figure 3 stamped on it, though whether it was among the ones I gave to Mr Templeman I cannot say.'

At this stage, the money recovered from the privy of Allen's house was produced, but no shilling stamped with the figure 3 was found.

The next witness to be called was Mrs Jane Lovett, of Northam's Buildings, Somer's Town. 'I was a tenant of the deceased. On Monday 16 March, Mr Templeman called upon me, by appointment, to collect his rent. I gave him the full sum of £3, made up of one half-sovereign, five or six half-crowns and the remainder in shillings and sixpences. I have since been shown the money produced at the Inquest today, but I could not identify it as having been that paid by me to Mr Templeman.'

Moving on, the Coroner addressed Inspector Miller. 'There was a small piece of wood produced at Hatton Garden that was picked up in the room where Mr Templeman's body was found. That piece of wood was supposed to have belonged to a larger piece missed by Mr Allen, the person who rents the cottage in which Gould lodged. This piece of wood was to be tested against another piece still in the possession of Mr Allen. I wish to know if that test has been completed and, if so, what the result was.'

Inspector Miller advised Whateley, 'The small piece of wood has been properly examined and has been found to be not of the same grain as the wood found at Allen's.'

Turning to Gould, Whateley asked, 'Are you desirous of calling up anyone to adduce evidence in your favour?'

'No Sir, I know of no one whom I can call up at present,' Gould replied.

'Do you wish to make any statement?' Whateley asked.

Gould appeared to hesitate, prompting the Coroner to state, 'You need not say anything unless you want to, but all you say will be taken down in writing.'

After a further lengthy pause, Gould declared, 'I would rather not make any statement at this time.'

Gould was led away in the custody of Mr Kilsby, the governor of the New Prison.

Mary Jarvis was then recalled by the Coroner and testimony was taken from John Ellis. Ellis added little to the testimony he had provided at the Inquiry, but said he had heard Mrs Jarvis, on hearing of the murder, say to Gould, 'You had better not go home.'

Mrs Jarvis immediately contradicted this, stating, 'That is not what I said, I actually asked Gould to come home with me, after I had met him by accident.'

With all the evidence having been presented, the Coroner dismissed Mrs Jarvis and addressed the jury. 'If you have made up your mind as to your verdict then there will be no need for me to sum up the evidence. If, however, your decision is not unanimous, it is my duty to go through and impress upon you the many and various points in the evidence. You should, therefore, consult together.'

After some consideration, the jury asked for all the evidence provided by the witnesses to be read over. After the reading, the Coroner again addressed the jury. 'You have now heard all the evidence that is likely to be obtained in this case. This can only lead to a conviction that a cruel and sanguinary murder has been committed by some person or persons. The object of this Inquest has been to determine who these persons are.'

'Regarding Mrs Jarvis,' Whateley said, 'I would not have felt it my duty to make any observation whatsoever in reference to her, had she not been brought to us as a prisoner, in custody upon the charge of being involved in the murder. The main fact borne against her throughout the case has been the discovery of a canvas bag, supposedly stained in blood, within her house. It has now been sworn to, in the expert evidence adduced by a Professor of Chemistry, that the spots on the bag were nothing more than iron based paint. It has also been discovered that the son of Mrs Tomkins had worn the bag as an apron and the paint had come from him being at Mr Harward's, the floor-cloth manufacturer and paper-stainer.'

'Taking all this into account,' the Coroner continued, 'I am disposed to ask what actual legal evidence there is against Mrs Jarvis. It is true there may have been an improper relationship between her and Gould, but there is no reason to conclude from this that she was an accessory to the murder of Mr Templeman and it certainly does not warrant the jury coming to such a conclusion.'

Whateley went on. 'The witness, Ellis, stated he had seen Mrs Jarvis going away from her home at 9am on the morning after the murder. Shortly after 2pm, he'd seen her again near the same place, in the company of Gould. When Ellis had asked the woman whether she had been home since he had first seen her and if she had heard of the stir created in the little village, she had said no.'

'I ask you to note,' Whateley said, 'that the witness, Ellis, firstly said that when he'd told Mrs Jarvis a murder had taken place, she had instantly responded, 'What, Mr Templeman?' Ellis had later qualified his statement, by revealing he'd also said to Mrs Jarvis the murder had involved the old gentleman residing in the cottage next to her. It is likely it was this additional information that had drawn the response, 'What, Mr Templeman?' from Mrs Jarvis. This demonstrates how careful people must be when repeating conversations, particularly in cases where the liberty, and possibly the life, of a fellow creature is at stake.'

'After she returned home, Mrs Jarvis had a conversation with Police-Sergeant Bradshaw and the policeman maintains she told him she'd heard nothing about the murder until she'd got home. This contradicts the evidence given by Ellis, but this contradiction is far from being of sufficient authority to connect Mrs Jarvis with the murder. Looking at the whole bearing of the case, in reference to Mrs Jarvis, the evidence against her is so slight and flimsy it is virtually impossible to think of sustaining it. Whether Mrs Jarvis had a guilty knowledge or not of the perpetration of the murder, we have no evidence whatsoever before us to establish a verdict of any description against her. Again, I must say, if she had not been brought before us in custody, I would not have thought it my duty to make any mention of her whatever regarding the case before us.'

'Regarding the prisoner Gould,' Whateley said, 'I am sorry to say the case bears a very different complexion. Throughout the entire evidence, Gould has not deigned to offer a single word of explanation, nor has he ventured to call any witness to disprove a single allegation.'

'Many people are disposed to believe circumstantial evidence is not sufficient to bring individuals to justice. I am utterly at variance with that opinion. I am of the firm view that a long and connecting chain of evidence can be efficiently exercised in tracing atrocious deeds to the guilty parties, in the absence of absolute proof.'

'It has, in this present case, been proved that on the Saturday and Monday prior to the murder, Gould had no money. He had told the potman, his friend, that he had but a penny. Then came the important evidence of the witness Jobson, who described Gould coming to his house and asking to see Jem. The witness stated Gould had informed him he required 'screws' and a 'darkey', as he was planning to 'serve out an old gentleman who lived in a lonely cottage'. Notwithstanding this evidence against him, coupled with the shrewdness which Gould possesses, not a single question did he put to the party by whom the testimony was provided.'

'Another interesting point is that Gould was found with a new pair of shoes on and he has declined to say where he obtained them, or what he has done with the old ones.'

'Then, we come to the sum of nine shillings found on his person,' the Coroner continued, 'which together with the money found concealed in the privy in one of his stockings and the money supposedly paid for the new shoes, comes close to the amount Mr Templeman was believed to have in his possession at the time of the murder.'

'There may be doubt in your minds as to whether the stocking found in the privy actually belonged to Gould, though there is strong evidence it did. It has been sworn to that the stocking had been seen only the day before the murder, on a box in the room in which Gould slept. With respect to the money, the facts show that on the Monday, the deceased received fourteen half-crowns from his friend in Skinner Street and five or six half-crowns from his tenant. This corresponds with the nineteen half-crowns found in the stocking.'

'Regarding the timeframe of the murder, it has been shown from the evidence that Gould left the Rainbow Public House at 11:40pm on the Monday night and he was not seen or heard from until between 2am and 3am on the Tuesday morning when he returned home. One would have thought it was within Gould's power to prove where he was and what he had been doing during that interval.'

'With all these facts before you,' Whateley declared, 'I fear you can come to no other conclusion than returning a verdict that would strongly inculpate the prisoner. I cannot adduce even one point in his favour, but that is entirely the fault of the prisoner, as he has not afforded the jury the slightest explanation, or offered them any evidence, of his own innocence.'

'If any other persons were involved in the murder, no evidence has been presented and I believe it would be inadvisable for the jury to return a verdict of wilful murder against some person or persons unknown. Under all the circumstances put before you, I believe it would be improper to mention Mrs Jarvis in your verdict.'

In conclusion, Whateley told the members of the jury, 'I shall now leave the case in your capable hands. I have absolutely no doubt you shall come to a conclusion that will satisfy your own consciences and meet the ends of public justice.'

The jury retired to an adjoining room to consider their verdict and after twenty minutes of deliberation returned to the Inquest room. The foreman passed a written verdict to the Coroner, which read: 'We, the jury, find Richard Gould, otherwise known as Arthur Nicholson, guilty of wilful murder upon the body of John Templeman.'

A murmur of approval spread around the room, as Richard Gould was formally committed to appear at the Central Criminal Court on the charge of wilful murder.

5 CHAPTER FIVE

Coroner's juries would later be largely phased out and they have rarely been used in England since the nineteen-twenties. The Coroner has retained the right to choose to convene a jury in any investigation, but in practice, it is very rare. Additionally, a Coroner's jury now only has the authority to determine the cause of death, its ruling can no longer commit a person to trial (that power was abolished as late as 1977).

On Tuesday 31 March, Mary Jarvis was formally released from custody.

The score on released prisoners had tied at 1-1, but the Coroner had won the race against the Police Magistrates to commit a prisoner for trial.

There was to be no triumphant walk to freedom for Mary Jarvis. As she left the Inquest, accompanied by her mother, she was spotted by a group of angry locals. The group pursued the two women down Little Saffron Hill. Observing the old saying, 'sticks and stones can break my bones but words can never hurt me', the mob added a volley of missiles to the volley of insults they unleashed.

As the chase continued into Little Warner Street, Mary Jarvis spotted the sign swinging above the Coach and Horses Public House and the two frightened women rushed into the pub to seek refuge from their pursuers. The crowd pushed their way inside, but the pub landlord quickly picked up on the rising tension and hustled the two women into a back room. Once he had secured the room, the landlord sent his son to the local police station-house to request assistance.

Inspector Penny, of G Division, immediately dispatched every available officer to the Coach and Horses. The policemen had some difficulty pushing their way through the increasingly hostile crowd that had now assembled, but eventually, they reached the room holding the two cowering women.

After they had checked Mrs Jarvis and her mother had not been harmed, the police set about clearing everyone else out of the pub and into the street. A protective cordon was formed around the two women as the police made the, literally, painfully slow journey from the public-house to the police house, through the hail of stones and mud raining down upon them. As the scene unfolded, John Jarvis, his child in his arms, could be seen observing from the sidelines.

The journey stalled at Crawford Passage and the bruised and mud-spattered policemen were relieved to see reinforcements arrive to drive the mob back. Eventually, Mrs Jarvis and her mother were hustled into the station-house, though the throwing of missiles continued unabated, with the target now being the station-house windows.

Having reached the sanctuary of the police station-house, Mrs Jarvis quickly regained her composure and expressed her determination to regain custody of her child. Though impressed by her stoic approach to the situation in which she found herself, Inspector Penny warned Mrs Jarvis he feared for her safety and asked if she had somewhere she could go.

Penny had the street outside the station-house cleared before a cabriolet he'd ordered arrived to whisk Mary Jarvis and her mother to an unknown destination.

The trial of Richard Gould, at the Central Criminal Court, began on 14 April 1840. Mr Chambers appeared for the defence and Messrs Jones and Ballantyne for the Crown, before Justice Littleton and Baron Alderson.

Gould faced the lengthy charge of, 'having, on 17 March last, in the parish of St Mary's, Islington, in and upon John Templeman, feloniously, wilfully and with malice aforethought, made an assault and that he, with a certain piece of wood, did inflict upon the said John Templeman, mortal wounds, blows, strokes and contusions upon his head, face and breast, of which mortal wounds, blows, strokes and contusions he did, there and then, die.' Whew!

Mr Jones opened for the prosecution and addressed the jury. 'I am anxious to place before you, fairly and dispassionately, the circumstances connected with this most atrocious and mysterious murder. The only objective the prosecution has in view is to bring the guilt home to the guilty party. I am sure if the evidence we propose to bring forward points to the prisoner as the guilty party, then you will not hesitate to do your duty, however painful it may be. If on the other hand, you should see reasonable grounds for believing the prisoner is not guilty of the atrocious act imputed to him, you should at once acquit him of the charge.'

'The unfortunate deceased,' Jones said, 'was an old gentleman. Although robust and athletic in his youth, latterly his frame had been debilitated by illness. He inhabited a cottage in a place called Pocock's Fields, near the Holloway Road, in the parish of Islington. Although several cottages were scattered around, the spot was, nevertheless, exceedingly lonely. The deceased slept and lived by himself, but a woman who lived close by was in the habit of occasionally attending upon him, to run errands and perform the duties of a domestic in his cottage.'

'A man named Jarvis and his wife lived in a cottage nearby, and another was occupied by a person named Thornton and her family. The deceased had the reputation amongst his neighbours as being a man of property and unfortunately for him, he appeared to have encouraged this notion.'

Jones then went on to narrate the facts pertaining to the murder of the deceased, laying out how the murder was discovered, the finding of the body, the state in which the cottage was found and the suspicious circumstances leading to the apprehension of the prisoner, on the night following the murder.

The first witness to be called was Elizabeth Thornton, who restated the evidence she had provided at the Inquiry and Inquest.

'How far is your cottage from Mr Templeman's?' Mr Chambers asked Elizabeth under cross-examination.

'It may be about a yard, as far as I can call to mind. It faces it. Our door is not opposite his door, it is about as far from it as from me to the bench of this Court,' Elizabeth replied.

'And where, relative to your own cottage, is the open window you discovered in Mr Templeman's cottage?'

'The window, which was open, looks towards our cottage. There is no yard before it, it is all one piece of ground, though there are palings all round our house and Mr Templeman's too. Our bedroom window faces towards Mr Templeman's. I recollect there was a pane of glass broken for some time in Mr Templeman's window. There was a piece of paper over it when my mother used to go backwards and forwards, but there was not that morning, it had been thrust through.'

'Are there any other cottages that directly neighbour Mr Templeman's?'

'There are three cottages within about the same distance of Mr Templeman's as ours. There are four cottages standing together, Jarvis's, ours, Mr Templeman's and Mrs Downes's. Mr Mustow's cottage is at the back, which makes five.'

'Did you see any footmarks outside the open window?'

'It was a beautiful moonlit night the night before I went, I think it was frosty. The ground was dry by the window where I was standing, it was more like clay than gravel. I think it was soft, but I did not look to see if there were any footmarks. I went home directly and told my mother,' Elizabeth answered.

Elizabeth's mother, Mary Thornton, was next up. After hearing her testimony, Mr Ballantyne asked, 'Did you see any money that day at Mr Templeman's cottage?'

'Yes,' Mary replied, 'he showed me some and told me he had received it in rent. It was silver and was in a little mahogany box. I had never seen the box before. He put it on the table to show me the money.

The table stood in the middle of the room. He had never shown me any money before.'

Under cross-examination, Chambers put to the witness, 'You have said today that you have seen the prisoner serve Mr Templeman with beer, is that quite correct?'

'Yes,' Mary replied. 'I never said I thought I had,' she continued when pressed by the prosecutor, 'well, I might have said so, but I can say now I did see him and that will settle it.'

When further pushed on the matter, Mary spluttered, 'I might have said I thought it, although I was certain. The prisoner used to come around to serve the neighbours with beer. It was seldom I had any beer myself, but when I did, it was Gould who served me.'

'Have you taken any strangers into your home, or are you aware of any of your neighbours having done so?' Chambers asked.

'I do not take lodgers, we have no room for ourselves hardly. Mr and Mrs Downes live in their cottage, she does not take lodgers, as far as I know. How should I know other people's affairs?' Mary protested.

As Chambers pressed further on the subject, Mary responded, 'I have not seen a strange man going in and out of Downes's cottage, to my knowledge, unless it was an acquaintance, who would be a stranger to me anyway. I do not know what sort of people they are, I never trouble my head about it. I saw people go in there, but I do not trouble my head with the concerns of my neighbours. I have not seen any strangers going in and out of Mrs Palmer's, or

Mrs Mustow's. They might have had visitors, I never take notice of other people's affairs.'

Next up was Francis Capriani. 'I am a night-watchman at Sadler's Wells theatre and live with my mother-in-law, Mrs Thornton,' Capriani said. 'I used to work for Mr Templeman, digging in his garden. On Monday evening, the 16th of March, I received seven shillings from him for my labour, made up of six shillings and two sixpences. I received it at about a quarter or twenty minutes before six o'clock, to the best of my recollection. I know a man named Jarvis and I have seen his wife. I saw her, at about half-past four o'clock that day, come away from her cottage and go to Mr Templeman's cottage and stand just by the door, talking to him for, to the best of my recollection, five or ten minutes. I did not see what became of her then, I was busy at work and I did not take notice of which way she went.'

'You were the first person to be taken up on this charge, is that true?' Chambers asked.

'Yes, on Tuesday, between twelve and one o'clock. I was discharged the next morning before the Magistrate, no evidence was given against me. The magistrate said he discharged me without a stain on my character after I'd accounted for how I had passed my time. I brought forward the call-boy at our theatre, to prove I'd let him out at half-past three o'clock.'

In response to further questioning, Capriani stated, 'I rent the cottage myself, but keep my mother to look after it. I do not know if Mr Templeman kept any tools in his house. He called me in that morning and sent me to fetch a basket of coals for him. He used to sit in the parlour, opposite the window. I never saw him sit with that window open.'

'When Mr Templeman paid you the seven shillings, did he take it out of a little mahogany box?'

'Yes, it stood on the table. I saw half-crowns, shillings and sixpences in it.'

'And when was this.'

'That was between a quarter and twenty minutes before six o'clock. I was not at home when the girl came to inform my mother-in-law of the window being open, I did not leave Sadler's Wells theatre till about five minutes to nine o'clock in the morning,' the witness replied.

William Kear, the first policeman on the scene, was next to provide his testimony.

'Exactly what time was it when you went to Mr Templeman's cottage?' Chambers asked.

'About twenty minutes after eleven,' Kear replied.

Under further cross-examination, Kear offered the following responses. 'I went at the request of Mr Roe, the surgeon. My beat is not in Pocock's Fields, it was normally P.C. Harris's beat. He went on duty at nine o'clock that morning and would usually continue there until two. I do not know who he relieved at nine, there was a man who left at nine. I do not believe that either of the men who were there that night and morning are here. I know Pocock's Fields, there are a great number of cottages there, principally inhabited by a working class of people. Mr Templeman's cottage is surrounded by other cottages.'

'Then you don't know who the men were. What is their beat, how far does it go?'

'It is called the Liverpool Road beat, it belongs to that beat.'

Responding to further questioning, Kear stated, 'I came on at nine o'clock that morning and was going off at two. I was at Highbury. I do not know how near the policeman in the Liverpool Road beat would have been to the place where this happened. I examined the deceased's wrists, but I did not observe them when the cord was taken off. I cannot tell whether the cord was put on after or before he was dead. He was bruised about the knees and on the breast. The pillow-case was covered in blood and it appeared he had received a blow while he was lying on the bed, judging by one of his teeth being on the pillow.'

Edward Roe, the surgeon, then testified and described his initial examination of the body and the crime scene.

'Did you find any teeth?' Mr Jones asked.

'I found one on the pillow, with a great deal of blood around it, and another on a chair, with a few spots of blood. I was present when a third was found by the policeman,' the surgeon replied.

Further examination by Jones elicited additional information from Roe. 'I examined the jaw and found three teeth had been forced from the sockets. They were not front, but side teeth. I think that was very probably done by the blow which produced the fractures. There were several blows about the mouth and I think one had been received while he was lying in bed, from the circumstance of the tooth being found on the pillow and the blood there. The tooth on the chair was as if it had fallen out when he got out of bed. I found a small piece of stick, about two inches and a half or three inches long, with hair attached to it and saturated with blood. It was hair from the head, dark hair, I can scarcely call it grey. This is the piece of splinter and as you can see, there is hair on it now. A kick from the heel or toe of a shoe might have made the cut on the nose if there were nails in it, and I think it might even be done by a shoe or boot without nails. From the appearance of the body when I saw it, I should judge the man had been dead for about five or six hours. The body had retained a little warmth about the region of the heart, though the rest of the body was quite cold. The time in which a body gets cold depends on the kind of death the person meets with. A body has retained warmth, occasionally, for up to two days after death. Ten or eleven hours is not at all an unusual time. I have no doubt that had it remained in the bed, the body would have stayed warm for a considerably longer time. Mr Lord accompanied me and he was also present at the post-mortem examination. The injuries which I saw on the body produced death and I have no doubt death was owing to the violence I have described.'

'How was the stocking fastened round the head?'

'It was tied in a knot, twice. The knot was formed in the stocking itself. The blow on the temple was above the stocking, over the temple,' Roe replied.

Chambers then began his cross-examination of the witness. 'Is it your judgment, as a man of experience, that the body had been dead for about five or six hours?'

'It is,' Roe replied.

In response to further questions, Roe offered, 'I should rather say a body would be more likely to retain heat for two days where the party came to his death by violent means. A body would, of course, be more likely to get cold on the floor than in bed. It was a very cold night on Monday and on the following morning too. I should think there were not more than sixteen ounces of blood altogether on the pillow and floor.'

'I believe the piece of stick you found is mahogany?' Chambers asked.

'I am no judge of wood. It is saturated with blood and the character of the wood is altered. It is splintered off a round stick, of that there is no doubt.'

Jones then re-examined the witness, to ask, 'In your judgment, would the blows you saw on the deceased occasion instant death?'

'I believe the blow over the left temple would occasion instant death,' Roe replied.

Responding to further questions, Roe said, 'I did not observe whether there was any matting or carpet on the floor. Mr Templeman might have been dead more than five or six hours, it is merely a matter of opinion. I saw nothing to render it improbable he had been dead a longer time.'

Seeking clarification, the Judge asked, 'It may have been fifteen, ten, or five or six hours, but it must have been at least five or six, is that what you mean?'

'Yes, it could not have been less than five or six. I do not know whether it might have been fifteen, it is a very difficult question to answer.'

Roe's fellow surgeon, Alfred Lord, was then called. 'I am a surgeon and live in Trinidad Place, Islington,' Lord said. 'I was present at Mr Templeman's cottage with Mr Roe and saw the state in which the body was found. I attended the post-mortem examination. In my judgment, the deceased died of the wounds I saw. The blow on the left temple would alone be sufficient to produce death. It produced concussion of the brain and extravasation of blood. He would not be able to stir after that.'

'Did the deceased appear to be an athletic, strong man?' the Judge asked.

'He appeared to have been so at one period of life,' Lord replied. 'From my observation of his body, he was rather a stout man and one who would struggle a good deal, I think. The hands were blue below the cord, both the hands and nails. I do not think one man could have tied his hands unless another had held them.'

The next witness to be called was Police-Sergeant John Collins. 'I went to Mr Templeman's cottage on Tuesday morning and was there with the surgeons. I have produced the splinter of wood and have had it examined, according to the prisoner's request, by a turner, who gave his opinion that it is 'Red Sanders'. He described it as a very heavy wood. I searched the drawers in the deceased's sitting-room. The top drawer on the left-hand side had been broken open, apparently by a chisel or small crow-bar. In the drawer, I found two boxes, papers and two notes of the Bank of Elegance, one for £50 and the other for £5. This is the mahogany box. It has a lock that has not been broken. It was shut when I found it but unlocked. I found the key for the box in the deceased's trouser pocket. I do not think any violence had been offered to the lock.'

Collins continued. 'I found no loose money in the drawers, but in Mr Templeman's trouser pocket, together with the key, was a purse containing three sixpences. Behind the door of the sitting room, I found a chopper and a hammer in the corner, between the outer door and the bedroom door. I do not think they had been used. I also found a hammer in the cupboard on the top of some clothes. That also did not appear to have been used. I found no piece of wood except this one.'

Under cross-examination, Chambers asked the policeman, 'How many persons have you taken up on this charge?'

'There have been four persons, Jarvis and his wife, Capriani and the prisoner,' Collins replied.

Further questioned, Collins said, 'Pocock's Fields is included in my duty. I was on duty on the Monday night, though I did not visit Pocock's Fields on my rounds. Thomas Peacock is the man who was on duty there, he is not in the courtroom today. I know Pocock's Fields well. I should think that Mr Templeman's cottage is a mile, or nearly so, from the Angel Public House, at Islington.'

'How far is it from the Rainbow Public House?' Mr Ballantyne asked.

'About a quarter of a mile.'

A new witness was then produced. 'I am Jane Lovett, the wife of Jonathan Lovett, and I keep an eating-house at 2 Northern Buildings, Somer's Town. We occupied the house as tenants to Mr Templeman. On Monday the 16th of March, Mr Templeman called on me at a quarter before twelve o'clock. I had known him for about three years. He appeared generally poorly in the winter, he had better health in the summer. He appeared rather poorly that day, he had a cold I should imagine. I paid him £3 that morning. It consisted of five or six half-crowns and one half-sovereign, with the rest in shillings and, to the best of my knowledge, sixpences.'

'Do you know where you got that money?' Chambers asked.

'I took it in from my business at different times. I took the whole of it within a period of two days in our shop,' Mrs Lovett replied.

'Did you observe whether Mr Templeman had any other money about him when you paid him the £3 for the rent.'

'No.'

'Where did he put the money you gave to him?'

'In his right-hand trouser pocket.'

Next in line to testify was Hannah Morgan. 'I live at 18 Skinner Street, Somer's Town. I knew the deceased, he called on me on the 16th of March at half-past eleven in the morning and asked me to lend him £3, which I did. I gave him fourteen half-crowns and twenty-five shillings. He gave me 1/- for a piece of mutton, to carry home to make him some soup. He dined with us and left at half-past three. He seemed in very low spirits and bad health, labouring under a very bad cold.'

'Did he give you any reason why he wanted to borrow the money?' Mr Jones asked.

'He said he wanted it to make up an account of money. He left at a quarter before twelve o'clock, then came in again and dined with us afterwards,' Mrs Morgan replied.

'Did he ask you to lend him the £3 before he went away the first time, or afterwards?'

'He asked for it as soon as he returned to dine, which was at about twelve.'

In answer to further questions from Jones, Mrs Morgan stated, 'I do not live near him. He left at half-past three in the afternoon. Skinner Street leads into the New Road, nearly opposite Judd Street. I cannot tell how far that is from Pocock's Fields, I was never there, only at the Barnsbury Castle Public House. I suppose it is two miles from there. I know Mrs Lovett, she lives about three doors from me. Mr Templeman gave me the shilling after he had asked for the £3.'

John Bush was the next in the long line of witnesses. 'I am a labourer and live in Goodwin Street, Barnsbury Park. I had a cottage in Pocock's Fields, called 'Spring Cottage'. About seven months ago, the deceased offered me £25 for it. He never brought any money forward and we did not come to any agreement at that time. I saw him about a week or nine days after, there was an agreement between my wife and him, and he said he would give me £25 for the cottage if I would take it. I said £25 was not enough and that I wanted £30. We only had one conversation on the subject, which took place at his own gate. I stood outside and he stood inside. I mentioned to several people about the conversation that had taken place between Mr Templeman and myself about the cottage.'

'This conversation took place between you and Mr Templeman alone?' Chambers asked.

'Yes, Sir,' Bush replied.

'How far from Mr Templeman's cottage do you live?'

'I suppose two hundred yards.'

Next up was John Mustow. 'I live in a cottage at the back of Mr Templeman's, close to his. I do not know the prisoner, but I have seen him about with beer from the Barnsbury Castle Public House, where he was employed as a potman. I cannot say how long it is since he left there. I know I took beer from him before Christmas, but I do not think I have since. I do not know whether he supplied Mr Templeman with beer. I have seen him about the cottages, supplying people with beer.'

'I knew Mr Templeman very well,' Mustow continued. 'I have heard he was in the habit of talking to people about his money and he has shown it to me several times. He has paid me small sums of money, which he generally took out of his pocket. He took out more than he needed, he appeared fond of showing his money. On the Tuesday before he was murdered, he showed me this £50 note. It was doubled up so I could just see the amount at the corner. It was in his room, he went to the drawer and fetched it out to show it to me. I did not mention the circumstance to anybody till after his death.'

Mustow's testimony continued. 'I saw the prisoner at Mrs Jarvis's during the time when he lived at the Barnsbury Castle Public House. I cannot say I have seen him there since, or anywhere else in the neighbourhood. I have two dogs. I keep one at the end of my house, where I keep my pigs, just at the back of Mr Templeman's cottage. It is always out at night, though I keep it chained up. He is a type of lurcher. Anyone he knows may do anything with him, but to strangers, he is not so civil. I kept that dog there while the prisoner was at the Barnsbury Castle. The prisoner was not acquainted with the dog. I do not think he knew him, he might have seen him, but not to be near him. I do not think the prisoner was ever on my premises.'

'When were you subpoenaed to attend here?' Chambers asked.

'Last night, that was the first time I was applied to,' Mustow replied.

'Did your dog make any noise on the night of the 16th?'

'No. The dog was about as far from the window at which the persons got into the house as the width of this Court, or half as far again. I am sure the dog would begin to bark at a stranger at that distance if he could hear footsteps, but it would be ten to one if the dog heard them because that window is in the front and the dog was at the back,' Mustow replied, concluding his testimony.

It was then the turn of Henry Wright to provide a statement. 'I am potman at the Duchess of Kent Public House, Devereux Street, Dover Road, where I have been working for the past seven weeks. It is about four miles from Mr Templeman's cottage. I have known the prisoner for some seven or eight months. I saw him on the 12th or 13th of last March, I am not positive which, I think it was the 12th, Thursday. He came to the Duchess of Kent at about half-past seven in the evening, called for a half-a-pint of porter and put down a penny, saying he had no more money. I did not take the money. I brought him a pint of porter and then went out to deliver my beer. I returned at about half-past eight. At that time, the prisoner was standing outside, opposite the pub, talking to a young man named Richard Squires. There was no further conversation between them after I approached.'

'We had some porter together,' Wright continued. 'As soon as we'd had the pot of porter between the three of us, the prisoner and I walked up the street together. While we were walking together, Gould said he'd been ill and was without money, and for want of money, he was getting worse. He said he knew of an old man who had money. I asked him how he knew this and he said he had heard the man had bid £25 for a cottage, then had flashed a £50 note and said if that was not enough he had more. The prisoner said the man had put the notes into a drawer and it would be a gift to him, for he knew where to put his hand on it. He then said he should like to have a 'right one' along with him. I said, 'A right one?' and he said, 'Yes, a right one or I could just do it myself.' I asked him where the old gentleman lived and he said, 'Oh, not far."

'Not far from where?' the Judge asked.

'Not far from where Gould lived.'

'Did he say so?' the Judge pressed.

'Yes, he said, not far from him. He said, 'Not far from home,' these were the words he used,' the witness spluttered, unconvincingly.

Mr Ballantyne then stepped in, to ask, 'Now, is that all you remember of what passed or was anything else said?'

'That is all I remember. He said nothing further than I have stated regarding the old gentleman's money.'

'Do you know where Mr Templeman lived?' Chambers asked.

'Yes, in Pocock's Fields, at the back of Liverpool Terrace,' Wright replied.

Upon further cross-examination, Wright explained, 'A sawyer lived in the next cottage to Mr Templeman's when I served him. I do not know who lives in it now. I think the sawyer's name was William Izod. He worked in the City. I served him beer, I served most of them near Mr Templeman's cottage, all round the field. I think there were not ten persons who did not deal with me when I carried beer round there. Nobody lived with Mr Templeman then and I do not know who took care of his house.'

Chambers continued to prod away at Wright's testimony and the cracks began to appear. 'I first knew the deceased when I was living at Mr Ralph's, the William the Fourth Public House, at the corner of Park Street and Minerva Place. I did not like it there and left because I got another position. There was no other reason for my leaving. After that, I went to the Craven Arms Public House, Bayswater. I was about twenty-six weeks at Mr Ralph's the first time and was eleven months at the Craven Arms. After leaving there, I went to work for Mr Ralph for a week, till he got a new man, and then I went to the Hope and Anchor Public House, Islington. The landlord left the pub and Mr Walton took it over. There were a few words between us and I left. There was no charge against me, the words were about stopping out for a few hours, I stopped out between four and eight o'clock.'

The tangled tale continued. 'I went away of my own accord. The words were with Mr Walton, who keeps the house. There had been no charge against me of any kind. Well, there had been a charge, but it was not from Mr Walton, it was from the Duke of York Public House, Gloucester Street. I asked permission to go out and, while I was out, a cash-box was lost. When I returned home, I was taken up on suspicion and charged with stealing it. That might be between four and five years ago, there has been nothing further. I never was in custody before, nor yet charged with anything. I lived in the City of London Public House, I was not in custody respecting anything there. It is at the corner of Sydney Street and Dalby Terrace. I left there to take a beer-shop, after nine years of service, I left of my own accord. There was a cellar there, nothing was said about my conduct in that cellar, that I swear. I opened the beer-shop before I went to the Duke of York Public House, but it failed. I know Mr Jarvis's cottage very well.'

'How long before the night Mr Templeman lost his life were you in Pocock's Fields, do you think?' Chambers asked.

'On the 9th or 10th I was there,' Wright replied.

As Chambers continued to push him, the witness revealed, 'I went to visit Mr Allen of Wilson Cottage, I had lodged there some time before. There are two rooms in Allen's cottage, plus an old back-kitchen and a wash-house adjoining it. There is about half an acre of garden. The privy is in the wash-house, adjoining the bedroom. You can go from the parlour into the little kitchen to get into it and you can go into the garden to get to it.'

'You mentioned something about what the prisoner said about a drawer in your statement at the Inquiry. Do you recall that?'

'Yes, I recollected that in my statement at the time I was at Hatton Garden, at my last evidence. I think I recollected it at the time I was at Hatton Garden, I am certain I did,' Wright stammered, before continuing. 'I have been twice to Hatton Garden, the first time was on a Saturday, the Saturday after Mr Templeman's body had been found on the Tuesday. I did not recollect it when I first went. I do not know anything of a little mahogany box. I am not positive I ever heard of a mahogany box. I have never mentioned it because I was not positive of hearing of it. I can read, I have read an account of this in the newspapers. I read the newspapers between my first and second examination. I did not read any account of where the money was kept.'

'On your oath, did you not read in the newspapers where the money was placed?' Chambers pressed.

'I have read the papers, but I speak from the words Gould said to me, that the money was in the drawer. I have no recollection of reading in the papers where the money was placed,' Wright replied.

The Judge interjected. 'What did you read the newspapers for, was it to refresh your memory?'

'No,' Wright responded.

Chambers pushed on. 'Was it a Sunday paper that you read?'

'I have read the Dispatch once, but not the whole of it,' the increasingly flustered witness replied. 'I think I read it the Sunday after my first examination, I do not know that I did, I am not certain that it was the Sunday after because in our business I catch hold of a paper and lay it down again. I did not read the whole account of the evidence, I had not the opportunity of doing so. I might have read part of it, I recollected about the drawer after I had been to Hatton Garden on the Saturday.'

'Had you mentioned about the drawer before you read the Dispatch?' the Judge enquired.

'No.'

'How old are you?' Chambers asked.

'Twenty-seven,' replied Wright, who was then faced with a further line of questioning, to which he responded, 'The last time I lodged at Allen's is about seven weeks back. I left Allen's to go to the situation I am now in. I was lodging there last Christmas and Gould lodged in the same house. He did not lodge there at Christmas, he was at Mr Bartlett's place, the Barnsbury Castle Public House, and he had been there for a week or two. I was living there alone at Christmas. I knew Mr Templeman's cottage and the window but never took particular notice of it. I cannot say whether it was a whole window, or whether there was anything the matter with it.'

'Were you aware that in the conversation which you say took place, a robbery was intended?' Chambers asked.

'Yes, I understood his intent was to commit a robbery, it was mentioned only in my hearing. I did not suppose any violence was to be done to the old gentleman. I understood him to mean, by 'a right one', somebody to assist him that he could depend upon. I understood there was to be a robbery only,' Wright replied.

'Were you shocked at it?'

'Why I took very little notice of it. I mentioned it to Squires when I went around at nine o'clock and said I did not know whether it was intended or not. Squires lives at the Two Brewers Public House, the next house. I did not mention it to any policeman. Squires said he did not think that if Gould had any real intention, he would have told me about it. Squires is not here today.'

'Did you think it was a joke?'

'I did not think he was joking, I just took no notice of what he said, till I named it to Squires at nine o'clock. Neither of us took any notice of it. It never entered my mind till I read, till I heard of the murder,' Wright spluttered.

'Why did you mention it to Squires if you thought nothing about it, and if you did think anything about it, why did you not mention it to a policeman?' Chambers pressed.

'I named it to Squires and it did not enter my mind afterwards, till Squires told me he had read in the paper of a murder. I read about it when I got home. I first heard of it on the Wednesday. Squires had read the paper and told me about it.'

Re-examining Wright, Ballantyne asked, trying to restore some credibility to his witness, 'You have been asked about a cash-box. Had some charge been made against you about it?'

'Yes,' Wright said, 'but it was only suspicion. I think I was in custody for a week. I was afterwards discharged by the Magistrate and did not come to trial upon it. Apart from that occasion, I have never been in custody in my life and I've never had any charge of dishonesty, or theft of any kind, made against me.'

'Did you give evidence in this case of your own accord, or were you called on to do so?' Ballantyne asked.

'I had not the time to come over. I sent word over to Mr Allen on the Wednesday, about an hour after Squires made the communication to me. I went before the Magistrate on the Saturday. One of the officers called to see me after I had made the communication to Allen. I stated at the office all the circumstances, as near as I could recollect. I never had any quarrel with the prisoner, I had always been on friendly terms with him.

6 CHAPTER SIX

Wright was finally allowed to step down and a new witness, John Richard Jobson, was called.

'I live at 7 Dorset Street, Spitalfields,' Jobson began, 'and I am a print-colourer. I colour caricatures, principally religious prints. I have known the prisoner for between four and five years. I saw him on Friday evening, the 13th of March. I left work at about half-past seven that evening and when I came downstairs there was a person in the passage enquiring for Jem. I did not see him at first, I heard him, and when I came down into the passage, the woman below said that Jem was not at home. It was then I saw the prisoner, Arthur Nicholson, at least that was the name he gave to me.'

'Nicholson was a private in the 11th Light Dragoons, based at Canterbury,' Jobson said, 'and he was present when I wrote the paper I have here in my hand, which states that if ever he should be tried as a deserter, I might know his real name. He gave me this, as near as I can recall, twelve months ago last December. He asked me to write down his name. I put the paper into a drawer and there it has remained until this occurrence took place.'

'When I saw him in the passage,' Jobson continued, 'I said, 'Dick, how are you getting on?' He said he wanted to see Jem and I asked him why. He said he wanted to see him so he could borrow a 'screw'. I asked him what for and he said he was going to serve an old gentleman in a lonely cottage. I told him he had better not do anything of the kind as if he did he would be sure to get transported. He told me he might as well be transported for that, for if he was taken as a deserter, he was sure to be transported anyway.'

Jobson went on. 'At the end of our conversation, a fight took place at the bottom of our street and the prisoner and I went down together to see it. Seven or eight rounds were fought. The police eventually came up to disperse the mob and the prisoner and I returned to my door before I wished him good night. He said, 'You had better not go yet, for I want to see Jem very particularly.' I asked him what he wanted to see Jem so very particularly for and he said he wanted a 'darkey' he had left there some time ago. I told him if he wanted to see Jem so very particularly, he had better go to the public-house. He said he could not go over the way, for he had no money. He further stated that if he served the old gentleman on the Saturday, as was his intention, he was going to go over the water to see his aunt or cousin and would give me a call on Sunday and let me know.'

'Let you know what?' Ballantyne asked.

'Whether he had robbed the old gentleman I suppose, that is the inference I drew from what he said,' Jobson replied.

'You have said he spoke about a 'screw' and a 'darkey', what is meant by a 'screw'?'

'I cannot tell, only from what I have been in the habit of reading. I have read 'Bell's Life in London' and I know what 'screw' means according to the definition I have read in the book. According to the definition I have read in 'Bell's Life in London', it means a picklock-key.'

'I bid the prisoner good night,' Jobson said, 'and we parted. I saw no more of him. I saw an account of the murder at Islington in the newspaper and, the day after, I gave information to a policeman of the H division. That division is in the neighbourhood of Spitalfields. I then stated to them what I have stated to you today, I believe, word for word. I was examined before the Magistrate after I had been taken by a policeman to identify the prisoner. Waddington, the jailer, said to me, 'Do you recognise the prisoner?' and I believe I said, 'Yes,' and I pointed to him, saying, 'that is the man.''

Mr Chambers stood to begin his cross-examination. 'How long have you known Gould?'

'Between four and five years,' Jobson replied, 'that was as near as possible my first acquaintance with him. I only knew him then as Dick or Richard, nothing further. That was at Mr Webber's, at the public-house at the corner of our street. I should say I knew him for three years as Dick.' 'Where was he living when he got you to write this card?'

'Why, I gave him a lodging, to tell you the truth, at 7 Dorset Street. I have not known him throughout the entire period of four or five years, he has been absent for some time. I had not seen him but once, before the Friday, for eight or nine weeks, that was at the Weaver's Arms Public House.'

'Who is this Jem to whom you refer,' Chambers asked.

'Jem is a person who had moved in below me,' the witness replied. 'His name is James Rogers and he had moved in very likely two months earlier. It is not my house, I am only the tenant of one apartment. I have known Rogers, I should say, for fourteen or fifteen years. It was not by my introduction he came into the room below, if I'd had the letting of the house, I would not have let him in at all.'

'You knew him too well?'

'No, I never knew of any dishonest action of the man, he is a labouring-man, he has only a small apartment at a rent of 1s 3d a week,' Jobson replied. 'He makes his living among the wharfs, on board the barges, to carry flour or corn, or anything on shore if barges come up and if they want anybody to unload them. They would as likely employ him as anybody else.'

'Does he have any regular employer?'

'He may have regular masters for all I know, but I do not know that he has.'

'What else has he been doing during the fourteen or fifteen years you have known him?'

'He made his living by going about buying and repairing old umbrellas, portering, or anything like that.'

'Is he often out late at night?'

'I do not know whether he comes in at good hours at night, he's never lived in the same house as me before. I had no objection to having him in the same house, but I have not the letting of the house.'

'Why would you object to having him in the house if you had the letting of it?' Chambers pressed.

'Because he is a man often out of work and he could not always afford to pay his rent,' Jobson replied.

'I have been in business for about twenty-four or twenty-five years,' the witness replied to further questioning, 'not always colouring religious prints, but latterly I have done them. I have done some thousands of prints for a Mr Fairburn, principally religious prints. I have occasionally done maps, plans and charts. That is the only trade I have been in, I never kept a shop. I have been eleven years in my present lodgings and have a wife and family living with me. I have three children and they live as well as they can since my work has been stopped. My work has been stopped since this fatal occurrence, I have had one little job since.'

'Why could you not continue to colour prints, notwithstanding this?' Chambers asked.

'Because I gave evidence,' Jobson replied. 'It got into the newspapers and my master stopped the work, I suspect so anyway.'

'Have you ever bought and sold items to make a living?'

'I do not buy and sell things at all, I never did to my knowledge. I bought this coat the other day and I might sell it tomorrow. I bought everything I have got on,' Jobson replied, defensively.

'Do not answer in that foolish way,' the Judge snapped. 'Did you ever buy and sell to make a profit?'

'No, never,' the chastened witness replied.

'So, you are saying you never bought anything to sell?' the dogged defence counsel asked.

'No, it was never said I did. I was never charged with buying anything.'

'Have you ever been arrested for robbery?'

'I was never in any scrape about a robbery, I am certain. I will tell you, the prisoner and I were together at a public-house when a man charged me with robbing him of a shilling. The prisoner went with me to the station-house and offered the man five shillings to let me out. I was not let out, but the man came back between one and two o'clock in the morning and said he had found the shilling. He wanted the police to discharge me, but they said they could not, as the charge for felony had already been signed. The man never appeared afterwards.'

'Where did this robbery incident occur?'

'It happened at the Bluecoat Boy Public House in Dorset Street, within a door or two of my own house. The man in question was a butcher. I have known him in the neighbourhood for years. That all took place not quite two years ago, I think.'

'Are there any other occasions on which you have been arrested?'

'I was once locked up for being drunk and disorderly, but I have never been in any difficulty about other people's property, except about the shilling.'

'When the prisoner said he was going to commit a robbery, did you endeavour to persuade him not to do so?' Chambers asked.

'I said if he did it he would be sure to be transported, but I did not endeavour to persuade him not to do it, I did not believe him,' Jobson replied.

'If you thought he really meant nothing, why did you tell him he would be transported if he did it?'

'Why he would if he did it, would he not.'

'Did you think he was joking?'

'I did not think he was in earnest, he has laughed and joked with me many times before.'

'Did you actually think he was joking, or did you think he was being earnest?'

'I firmly believe now that he did mean it, but I did not believe he meant it at the moment. I should sooner say he was in joke than in earnest.'

'Why persuade him not to do it then, and tell him he would be transported?'

'All I said was that if he did it, he would be transported.'

'Now, while you were pausing to give me an answer, did you hear what that gentleman, Mr Ballantyne, said? Did you give me your answer after hearing what that gentleman said?'

'I did not hear what he said, I did not hear him speak. I could see his lips move, that is all,' Jobson pleaded.

Under further cross-examination, Jobson stated, 'I did not shake hands with the prisoner when I parted with him. I have shaken hands with him many times. I did not see Jem that night, nor tell him he was wanted. I left the prisoner at the door when I bid him good night. I did not go up to my own room. I came back between eleven and twelve o'clock, I believe. I do not know whether Jem was at home. I did not see Jem at all before I read something in the newspapers.'

Mr Jones then rose to re-examine the witness. 'Had you any other reason for not liking to have Jem in the house, other than his poverty?'

'No, that is the only reason.'

'Have you ever been in custody, other than on the matter you described to us today?'

'No, Sir, only on the occasion I have mentioned.'

'You have been asked whether you believed the prisoner was serious when he said he was going to commit a robbery, did you believe it at the time?'

'So many jokes have passed between us, I did not know how to take it. I believe it now, from what has happened,' Jobson responded.

'At what time was it that he came to you?'

'About twenty minutes to eight, as near as I can recall. At half-past seven, I sent my wife home with three hundred prints. I had just got my coat and shoes on and came down, so I judge it to be at that time.'

The witness completed his testimony by stating, 'He was with me altogether for about a quarter of an hour. He left me before eight o'clock. As I passed the station-house to go into Church Street, the bells struck out eight and that was the moment I had parted with him. I did not see Jem during all the time I was with the prisoner.'

Next up was the mysterious Jem Rogers. 'I am James Rogers and I live at 7 Dorset Street, Spitalfields. I am an umbrella maker by trade, but I do not follow that line of work. I work at the water-side as a labourer. I have known the prisoner for about five years, or it may be six, by the name of Richard or Dick. The 13th of March was the last time I saw him, barring seeing him at Hatton Garden. I saw him at my door when I was going home between eight and nine o'clock in the evening.'

'Between eight and nine o'clock?' Ballantyne asked.

'Yes. I believe I once said a quarter before eight o'clock, but I now say it was between eight and nine,' Rogers replied.

'Where were you standing?'

'I was coming home and he was standing by the window as I was coming, just between the window and the door. The first observation he made to me was, 'Jem, you are just the chap I want to see.' I said, 'What do you want to see me for?' and he said, 'I want for you to lend me two 'screws' and a 'darkey'.'

'And what did you think he meant by that?'

'I should say he meant skeleton keys and a dark lantern. I said he might as well ask me for a £500 note as to ask me for such things as these. Nothing else was said on that subject.'

Continuing, Rogers stated, 'I said I had no money for beer, or else I would treat him, and he said he had none. My brother-in-law was along with me, he had not been with me all the time, but he came up along with me when I came to the door. I don't think he heard anything of what was said, but I cannot say whether he did or not. I said to my brother-in-law, 'Bill, would you stand a pot of beer,' and he said, 'I have not got any money without going home to fetch it, but go over to the public-house, call for a pot of beer and I will come and pay for it.' We then went to the Bluecoat Boy Public House in Dorset Street and had a pot of beer.'

'Why would the prisoner have come to you for 'screws' and a 'darkey'?' Mr Chambers asked.

'I once kept an old iron shop,' Rogers said, 'that was while I was acquainted with the prisoner, and he knew it.'

'Where was it that you kept the old iron shop?'

'In Little Paternoster Row. I did not keep the property, I had the lower part for nine or ten months, then necessity compelled me to leave it. I sold locks and bought and sold old iron and sometimes bottles and rags. I did not just take anything that came to hand because there might be things that came in a different sort of way. I was very careful of what I bought. I used to go and collect things. I mostly bought in Petticoat Lane. I have never been in any scrape arising from the old iron shop, not at all. I was never taken up, though if I were to say I never was in any prison, I should say false. When I was a boy, I got a month for sleeping out in the open air, that was seventeen or eighteen years ago. I had no work then. I was sent to Coldbath Fields for a month, I cannot recollect anything else.'

Replying to further questions, Rogers said, 'I became acquainted with the expressions 'darkey' and 'screws' by reading 'Bell's Life' newspaper. I don't know whether Jobson reads it. I am sure I have seen those expressions in 'Bell's Life'. I never read it in 'Tom and Jerry', I do not know that I ever took up that paper. I have known Jobson, I suppose, for about ten years. He lodges in the same house as me, with his wife. He has got three or four children I believe, I very seldom go up into his room. I believe he was a print-colourer when I first knew him. I may have been up in his room two or three times.'

'How long before Gould visited you, had it been since you had seen Jobson?' Chambers asked.

'I suppose not for a month, I go in and out of the place. I live downstairs. I have not lodged there altogether, I believe, above four months. I have seen Johnson outside of the house, but not in the house, to my knowledge.'

In answer to further questions from Chambers, Rogers stated, 'My brother-in-law's name is William Crane. Crane was with me, then he went home to get the money, returned and paid for the beer, and then retired to look after a sweetheart of his. He was standing within a yard or two until he went away to get the money. The prisoner did not whisper, he spoke loud enough so Crane might or might not have heard what he said, I cannot say for sure.'

Under further cross-examination, Rogers said, 'I had no notion what the 'darkey' or 'screws' were wanted for, I never gave it a thought. There had been no 'darkey' left with me at any time. I did not see Jobson at all that night, I do not think I saw him at all afterwards until I had been up to Hatton Garden, though I am not positive.'

'I never kept such things as skeleton keys when I was in the iron trade,' Rogers claimed, 'nothing of the kind, nor dark lanterns.'

'Did you think there was anything wrong in the prisoner asking for these?' Chambers asked.

'I did not give it a thought whether there was anything wrong or right, I did not trouble my head about it and I passed it off as a joke.'

Re-examining the witness, Ballantyne asked, 'Were you compelled to go before the Magistrate, or did you give evidence voluntarily?'

'I saw the story in the paper,' Rogers replied, 'and I went up to Hatton Garden the same day, but there was no Court session that day. It was not the same day that I saw the account of the murder, but the same day I saw my own name in the paper. That was on the Monday. I went up that same day, but the examination was not on. It restarted the following day and I attended and gave evidence then. I stated everything I knew.'

'When you went to be examined, did you know Jobson had already appeared?'

'I was told he had appeared the week previous, but I did not see Jobson until after I had been examined. I think I may have read about his examination in the newspaper before I was examined, but I cannot be positive' Rogers replied, concluding his testimony.

The next witness to be called was Richard Squires, who declared, 'I am a waiter at the Two Brewers Public House, George Street, Horsemonger Lane, and have been so four years. I know the prisoner, but I have met him no more than three times in my life. I saw him last, I think, on the 17th of March. He came over the water to see Wright. It was on the Thursday evening to the best of my recollection, at about half-past eight in the evening, or it might have been nine o'clock. I saw him close by where Wright lives, at the Duchess of Kent Public House, though he was not with Wright at that particular time.'

'I know Wright,' Squires said, 'and have been out drinking with him from time to time. We drank together that evening, Wright, Gould and me. I believe I left first and went straight home.'

'Did you go straight to bed?' Ballantyne asked.

'After I had done my business,' Squires replied. 'I had to wait on the company in the tap-room. I did nothing more, though I saw Wright again, I believe, that night, at the Duchess of Kent Public House, where he lives.'

'Did you have any further conversation with Wright when you saw him again if you did see him?'

'I do not know whether it was the same evening or the next morning, it might have been the next morning I saw him. I believe he mentioned Dick's name, but I cannot recall what he said,' the seemingly amnesia-stricken witness replied.

'Who came for you today?' Ballantyne asked, in the vain hope the short-term memory of the witness might be stronger than his long-term memory.

'I do not know his name,' Squires replied, 'he just said I was wanted here, but he did not mention for what. To my knowledge, he did not tell me what I was wanted for, he just said I must come to the Old Bailey or something of that sort. He told me he wanted me to come along with him, though he did not say anything about what it was about, nothing at all.'

'Do you mean to swear you had no idea what you were going to be examined about before you went into that box?' Ballantyne asked, fixing the witness with an incredulous glare.

'Yes, I knew what it was about, I was up at Hatton Garden before, but my evidence was of no use. I was not examined. I stated what I knew and it was of no use.'

'You stated what you had got to say at the Inquiry and then you were sent away?' Mr Chambers asked, seeking some clarification before beginning his cross-examination.

'Yes.'

'I came here today in a cab, with one of the servants, I expect, from this office.' Squires stated. 'He found me at the Two Brewers Public House. I had very little conversation with him on the way. I have not seen Wright here today, but I heard him examined at Hatton Garden the last time. He and I have talked about the matter since then, we have sat together and talked.'

A somewhat over-optimistic Chambers asked Squires to recount the details of his meeting with Gould and Wright.

'When I went up, I found Gould standing near the Duchess of Kent Public House. Wright was not there then, he came up about half a minute after I met Gould. I cannot say what was said while we were talking together, nothing very particular. We drank a pint of porter, or whether it was a pint or a pot I cannot say. We drank it at the opposite corner to the Duchess of Kent, where Wright lives, I mean outside the Duchess of Kent. We were about three minutes together there, it might be four. We did not talk much, we continued drinking till the pot was done. No one paid for the beer at that time, we had some beer out with us from my house and from the Duchess of Kent. I was carrying beer out, though I cannot say whether the pot was taken out of my beer or out of Wright's.'

The mind-numbing story continued, with even less detail. 'I cannot say how much was consumed. I cannot say whether it was a pint or a pot. I cannot swear whether it was my master's beer, or Wright's master's beer, that we drank. I might have paid my mistress for it, I paid for all I brought out, but I cannot say how much I paid her. No money was produced by anybody while we were drinking and nothing was said about money, to my knowledge. I believe that, when I first saw Wright, he was coming along with his porter and I was talking with Gould.'

'When they saw each other, did they ask each other how they were, or what exactly was said?' Chambers asked, manfully sticking to the task.

'No, it appeared they had been together earlier. Wright might have said, 'Hello,' I do not know that he did, I cannot recollect anything that was said. The time might have been half-past eight or nine o'clock, I should say it was half-past eight, as near as I can recollect, because I was out with my porter. I go out with it at eight o'clock and I was just going home. I might have had some porter left, I generally have, I cannot say whether I had or not.'

'Did you toss for any porter?' Chambers asked, though the answer would have come as no surprise.

'We might have tossed, though I do not recollect tossing. We might have been a pint each or stood a pint, either one of us. I have no recollection whether we tossed, or whether we were a pint each, or whether one of us stood a pint. I cannot say we did not toss, we might have tossed and I've forgotten it.'

'What happened after you had finished drinking?' the barrister asked wearily.

'I immediately went in and was waiting on the customers after that,' Squires said. 'I came out again that night with beer. That would have been at nine o'clock if it was half-past eight before. If it was after nine o'clock, I would not have come out. I do not sleep in the house, I sleep with my wife, in St. George's Court, Dover Road. It might have been twelve o'clock when I went home. I cannot recollect when I went home that night. I cannot recollect who I saw when I was going home.'

Mr Ballantyne put a couple of further questions to the witness. 'You were taking out beer for your mistress, what is the method you use? Do you account for the number of pots you take out?'

Squires replied, 'I have to pay for all the porter I take out every day, I never return any, I pay for all every night. I live two-hundred or three-hundred yards from the public-house I work at. I cannot swear whether I left that night before or after the house was closed.'

With that, to the great relief of everyone in the

courtroom, the befuddled witness was excused.

7 CHAPTER SEVEN

It came as some relief to next hear the testimony of a familiar witness from the Inquest and Inquiry, Charles Allen, who outlined how he had become suspicious his lodger, Richard Gould, had been involved in the murder of John Templeman. Allen's testimony, thankfully, varied little from that he had given at the earlier hearings.

After Allen had finished providing his statement, Mr Ballantyne asked him, 'Have you told us the entire conversation, as far as you recollect, that took place between you and the prisoner on the subject of the murder?'

'Yes,' Allen replied, 'as far as happened, except the part where my wife was speaking to him. There was a conversation on Scripture and I recollect, in one part, Richard said if the Ten Commandments were just, or the Mosaic Law was right, he had broken them all. Then that conversation dropped with me and went on with my wife. I got up to go into the yard. This was at the time we were talking about the murder.'

'Did any of the money that was later found in your house belong to you?'

'I saw some money produced in a stocking at the station-house at Islington. Neither the money nor the stocking was my property. I believe one farthing was all the money I had in the house that day. I have never been in the habit of keeping money in the wash-house or privy, we have not had any reason to do so.'

Mr Chambers then asked, 'Were you present during all the time your wife was in conversation with the prisoner that evening?'

'Certainly not,' Allen retorted, 'I went out to fetch some beer and bacon and therefore I could not have heard everything.'

'Up to that time, had there been any conversation about the murder?'

'The conversation might have been about the murder, but I took very little notice of any of the conversation, therefore am not bound to answer the question.'

'Now, I ask you to answer the question, had any conversation taken place about the murder before, as you said in your testimony, you noticed the prisoner's new shoes?' Chambers pressed.

'I have already answered that the conversation when I entered the house was on that subject,' the slightly agitated witness replied, 'but I paid so little attention to the conversation between my wife and the prisoner, I could not utter fifty words of the conversation the whole evening. I mean, I could not utter fifty words of the conversation between the prisoner and my wife.'

'At the time you went out to fetch beer and bacon, did you suspect the prisoner had some involvement in the murder?'

'Certainly. I was suspicious at the time before he even came into the house.'

In reply to further questioning from Chambers, the witness stated, 'I was absent for about ten minutes or a quarter of an hour. On my return, I found the prisoner sitting at the table in conversation with my wife. As soon as his bacon was cooked, he had his supper, smoked his pipe and went to bed. I then bolted him in his bedroom and said to my wife, 'He is locked in, he shall never come out of any snore by me.' If my face had been towards him, I think he may have heard that, but my back being towards him, he might or might not, it is a question I cannot answer.'

'I had never bolted him in before,' Allen continued, 'I have merely put the bolt on to keep the children in, but not bolted him in. The window of his room looks into the front garden, it is about two feet and a half or three feet from the ground.'

The questions from Chambers continued to flow and Allen responded to each of them. 'I cannot tell whether he paid me for the old shoes I made for him. What I have no dealings with I never answer. I left it to my wife to collect the rent from him, he paid her in part and whether she had the whole I cannot tell. I have been ill this past year and have done very little shoe-making in that time. I was once in the police force. I left it, I think, some eight years ago. I was in it, as near as I can tell, for a year and four or five months. I left entirely of my own accord, without any complaint being made.'

'Why did you bar the bedroom door, I do not understand?' the Judge enquired.

'Because I had a suspicion he knew something of the charge and barring the door would prevent his getting out,' Allen replied.

'Could he not get out of the window?' the Judge asked.

'That he might,' Allen replied, 'but he could not get into my room and if he could have got out of the door, I did not intend to go to sleep.'

'Were you afraid of him,' the Judge pressed. 'I was not particularly afraid of him, but I did not intend he should have gone out of my house, for the public interest as well as my own.'

Charles Allen was then followed by another familiar witness, his wife Mary, who declared, 'The prisoner lodged at our house and did so on the 17th of March last. I do not know Mr Templeman's cottage, I never saw it. I know it is but a short distance from our house, I have never been to it, but I know where it is. The prisoner has been lodging with us for nearly a year, off and on. The last time, he was with us for a whole week, the only full week he has been with us since he had been at the Barnsbury Castle Public House. He was with us from Saturday night until the Tuesday week, a week and two days. He did not pay me. I never received any money from him for rent that week, because he had none. He told me many times he had no money.'

'Did he not pay you at any time during the year?' the Judge asked.

'Yes, he paid me whenever he could,' Mrs Allen replied.

'When were you first aware the prisoner had suddenly come into money?' Ballantyne asked.

'I only knew when I saw the stocking in which the money was found in the privy.'

'Do you know to whom that stocking belonged?' the prosecutor asked.

'I saw a pair of rolled up stockings on a box at the side of the prisoner's bed, on Monday afternoon, at the time I made the bed,' Mrs Allen replied, adding, 'I cannot say whether it was at five o'clock, or at what time it was. It was in the afternoon, it might have been five o'clock, while the prisoner was out. I took hold of the stockings and laid them down and thought to myself, these are Richard's stockings. I knew them to be the type he always wore.'

The witness continued to answer the questions put to her by Ballantyne. 'I washed for him. He had two pairs of stockings when I washed for him before he went to Mr Bartlett's. I had washed a pair of stockings like those ones for him, just before Christmas. That is all I know. My children's clothes were not kept in that room, nobody's clothes but the prisoner's would be kept in that room. They were two odd stockings, I had mismatched them when I washed them. I think it must have been six weeks before Christmas when I mismatched them. They were formerly two pairs and I put one stocking of one pair to one of the other pair.'

'But he could have rightly matched them afterwards?' the Judge interjected.

'He never did while I washed for him because they came off together and were washed together,' Mrs Allen answered.

'Do you remember his coming home wet-footed one day?' Ballantyne asked.

'When he was out with baked potatoes one day, he came home wet in the feet and I gave him a dirty stocking to put on, a dry one. That is how they became mismatched,' Mrs Allen replied. 'As soon as I saw the stocking in which the money was found, I said it was the one I had seen,' she continued. 'I knew it belonged to Richard and was on the box on the Monday, I am quite sure of that. I am quite sure it was the same stocking I had seen by the side of the bed on the Monday.'

'Who washed for him when he returned to lodge with you for the week?' Mr Chambers asked.

'I do not know,' Mrs Allen replied, 'his dirty things were not sent to the wash. I never saw any in the house, they were not put up in a bundle. I have no recollection of saying anything about the stockings being in a bundle, they were rolled up in the ordinary form of a pair of stockings, one doubled over the other.'

'How much did the prisoner pay you for rent?' Chambers asked.

'When he was in employment, he paid me 2/- per week. We never made any agreement this time, I knew he was out of employment and never asked him for anything. If he had gained employment, I should have expected the same weekly sum.'

'When did your husband first remark about the prisoner having new shoes?' the defence counsel asked.

'When Richard came in during the evening.'

'I thought your husband was out when the prisoner came in.'

'My husband was out, but Richard had stood talking to me by the table and had not sat down by the time my husband came in.'

'Was it in consequence of your husband noticing he had new shoes that the prisoner said he'd got them from his cousin?'

'I do not know, but he did say that. I did not ask him about the shoes. My husband looked at them and so did I, but I never asked where he got them. He said he had been very lucky that day.'

'Was it not afterwards that the prisoner talked so despondently about being such an unlucky man?' Chambers asked.

'No, it was during that same conversation.'

Re-examining the witness, Ballantyne asked, 'Did you unroll the stockings by the bedside?'

'No,' Mrs Allen replied, 'I merely took them in my hand. There was a pair of stockings on the box on the Monday and I am quite sure it was the outside stocking that the money was tied in.'

'How could you tell there were two odd stockings?' the Judge asked.

'I said to the policeman, 'There is a pair of stockings,' then the policeman found the other stocking in my room, behind the box. They were two odd stockings and I said I had mismatched them when I washed them,' Mrs Allen replied, concluding her testimony.

The next batch of witnesses to be produced were intended to establish the whereabouts of Gould on the night of the murder.

John Frimley, the landlord at the Rainbow Public House, stated, 'I know the prisoner. On Monday, the 16th, he was at the Rainbow for most of the afternoon and he stayed until twenty minutes before twelve o'clock at night. I did not actually see him coming into the Rainbow that afternoon, I first saw him at about four o'clock. He was playing at skittles until the gas was turned out in the skittle-ground at a little after ten. He then came into the tap-room and he remained there until twenty minutes before twelve. He then left, in the company of the others that were there. On the following day, Tuesday, I saw him at the Rainbow between two and three o'clock in the afternoon. I last saw him, in the tap-room, at seven o'clock. I believe he was there after seven, but I last saw him at seven.'

Chimney-sweep Robert King testified next. 'I was at Frimley's skittle-ground on Monday evening, the 16th of March. The prisoner was playing there. He'd began playing at about half-past seven or eight o'clock. When he first came into the ground, he said he only had three halfpence in his pocket and if either of us would bet odds or evens he might have enough for a pint, but nobody would bet against him. He then played at skittles for a pot of beer, I believe. I think it was very nearly eleven o'clock when we came out of there. I know he did not lose anything because I was there all the time. He did not win any money, he won beer. I went into the tap-room with him afterwards.'

Next in line was Robert Pizey, who stated, 'I live at 17 Elder Walk. I was in the skittle-ground of the Rainbow Public House on Monday the 16th of March and saw the prisoner there. I afterwards went into the tap-room. I was going out for some tobacco when the prisoner asked me to fetch him a rush-light. He gave me two halfpence, so I bought one and gave it to the prisoner.'

Last up in this little group of witnesses was Mary Elizabeth King. 'I am the wife of Robert King. I was at the Rainbow Public House on the 16th of March. I went there at about twenty minutes to twelve, to fetch my husband. I saw the prisoner there. I remember the gas being turned off, though the people did not all come out together. I went out first and they came about five minutes afterwards. I observed the prisoner particularly, he had on a fustian coat, the same one that he has on now.'

Mrs King continued. 'I noticed it because I saw something in his right-hand pocket. It must have been about a quarter to twelve when I noticed it, at the time he was going away. The instrument was the length of his pocket. It was lying long ways in his pocket, across the bottom. The ends seemed to be different. I saw this when he turned his back to the fire-place. After we came out, my husband and I went one way and the prisoner went along towards the Chapel of Ease, which lies in the direction of Mr Templeman's cottage.'

Police-Inspector James Miller was the next witness to be called, as the long day in Court continued. 'I am an Inspector of the N division of police. I apprehended the prisoner at Allen's cottage on Tuesday night, the 17th of March, at a quarter after eleven o'clock. I found him in the bedroom, in bed with two children. I roused him and said, 'Gould, get up and dress.' On getting out of bed, he said, 'Where is your warrant?' I replied, 'I don't need a warrant.' He then said, 'What do you want me for then?' I said, 'I suppose you have heard of the murder, it is that I want you for.' He smiled and said, 'If I was as innocent of everything as I am of that, I should not have much to fear.' I do not recollect his saying anything more.'

Miller went on. 'As he was packing up his clothes to dress, I found nine shillings in his trouser pockets. In his waistcoat pocket, I found seven Lucifer matches and two receipts, one for a pair of trousers in the name of Richard Gould and the other, for a jacket in the name of Ann Jarvis.'

'On the way to the station,' Miller continued, 'Gould said a pot-boy at the William the Fourth

Public House had taken a warrant out against him for an assault and it was that he'd supposed I was after him for. I searched him at the station-house and took from his feet a pair of new shoes or ankle boots. I asked him where he'd bought them and he said, 'In Kent Street.' I then asked him what he had done with his old ones and he replied he had thrown them away.'

'Shortly after that, I minutely examined his clothes and took from him this waistcoat, which he was wearing at the time. He had three waistcoats on, two besides this one. This was the middle one. I noticed at the time that this waistcoat was stained with blood and was burnt in one particular spot as if a cinder or a pipe had fallen on it.'

'Have you had the waistcoat examined to ascertain what exactly had made the stain?' the Judge asked.

'No, the waistcoat has not been subsequently examined,' Miller replied.

'Did you search the bedroom in which you apprehended the prisoner?' Mr Jones enquired.

'I did,' the Inspector replied, 'and I found this single stocking there. It was lying on a chair by the side of a box. I did not search any other part of Allen's premises, only the bedroom where I took the prisoner. I found the stocking about a quarter after eight o'clock on the Wednesday morning.'

'Did you observe how the prisoner's door was fastened?' Jones asked.

'It was bolted from the outside.'

Another policeman, Sergeant Thomas Hobbs King, was called next. 'I accompanied Police-Constable Bradshaw to Allen's cottage on the Wednesday morning. I searched the premises and found a stocking between the ceiling of the back-kitchen and the roof and tiles of the privy. I had to lean over and put my arm round behind the rafter. Seeing something white, I stood on the seat of the privy to reach it. It is a full five feet from the seat of the privy to the rafter and I should not think a short person could have put it there. Standing on the seat, a person as tall as the prisoner could, or someone as tall as Allen. I examined the stocking and found it to contain nineteen half-crowns, forty-eight shillings and seven sixpences.'

Ralph Wilcox, shoemaker, his daughter Hannah and John Walker, a boy who worked in the shop, were all called to testify as to the sale of a pair of shoes like those produced in Court, but none of them could swear as to whom the shoes had been sold.

With that, the case for the prosecution was concluded.

The marathon session of taking evidence was ended by Henry William Smith, a clerk at Horton's boiler and gas meter manufacturers, who provided a statement on the good character of the prisoner.

The long day's journey into night saw Mr Chambers address the jury, on behalf of the prisoner, at 10:30pm.

'The time has now arrived,' Chambers began, 'when it becomes my duty to endeavour to rescue an unfortunate young man from the mass of evidence and prejudice that appears to press him down, and under which no other feeling but one of perfect innocence could have sustained him.'

'The law of England requires the evidence against a prisoner to be unquestionable and unimpeachable. It forms no part of the criminal justice system that a prisoner, charged with an offence of this serious nature, should be required to account for all of his actions.'

'You, the jury, must be entirely satisfied the prisoner was the one who committed this most strange and atrocious murder before you can venture to pronounce him guilty. What was his conduct when the police arrived to apprehend him and in what situation was he found?' the lawyer asked, before providing his own answer. 'He was found sleeping beside two children. What was his answer on being told he was being charged with murder? Did he betray those appearances of conscious guilt a murderer would have done? No, his answer to the police officer was, 'I wish I were as innocent of everything else as I am of a charge such as this."

'I have to say,' Chambers declared, 'I believe the evidence produced today against the prisoner, to be the vaguest and most unsatisfactory to ever have been brought forward in support of a charge such as this. It has been categorised as circumstantial evidence, but, I ask you, was the chain so unbroken and so certain it could lead you to the inevitable conclusion the prisoner was the guilty man.'

'Where is the proof of guilt? The material witnesses for the prosecution appeared in the box, not to tell the truth, but to twist and conceal the facts to fit the prosecution's case. It is true the prisoner was found in possession of nine shillings at the time of his arrest, but although his previous poverty has been strongly insisted upon, there are no just grounds for assuming he did not come into possession of such a sum by fair and honest means. Why should it be inferred the money was part of the produce of this fearful and odious crime?'

'If the prisoner had hidden the money in the stocking found by the constable, was it not likely he would have concealed it all and not taken the risk of carrying part of it on his person? Again, if he was armed with a deadly weapon, was it likely he would have carried it to a skittle-ground in his pocket?'

'I ask you, having heard the evidence, are you of the opinion this murder was committed by one or more persons? One of the surgeons has suggested at least two people must have been involved. Who then was the other person? There is a good reason to believe the crime was committed by persons who have yet to be discovered and the prisoner has been made their scapegoat.'

'If it could be proved the prisoner had been found watching the premises of the deceased prior to the murder, then there might be reasonable suspicion against him, but his whole conduct and demeanour, from the time of his apprehension down to the present moment, has been that of a man perfectly conscious of his innocence, at least for the crime of murder, whatever other offences might be laid at his door.'

'This case is one of a most extraordinary and mysterious circumstance,' Chambers ventured. 'The supineness evinced by the neighbours of the murdered man, after the discovery of his mangled remains, is a singular feature in the case. Some of these people, without doubt, know well who the guilty parties are, but, although this case has already occupied so many hours, nothing has transpired to fix guilt upon those who actually committed the murder, for, that the prisoner had no hand in it, must, by this time, be quite apparent to all who have heard the evidence presented by the prosecution.'

Continuing his tactic of deflecting responsibility from the accused, Chambers claimed, 'This case clearly requires further investigation and it can only be hoped the actual perpetrators of a murder so foul and barbarous shall yet be brought to justice.'

Chambers then reviewed the evidence and contended it would not be safe to lend credence to the statements made by most of the witnesses. Neither Allen nor his wife was to be trusted, the barrister claimed, as their conduct in the affair was, in his opinion, exceedingly suspicious. He then ventured no reliance whatsoever could be placed upon those witnesses who had endeavoured to fix guilt upon the prisoner by detailing conversations they'd had with him regarding 'screws' and a 'darkey'. The defence lawyer concluded by informing the jury he was happy to leave the fate of the prisoner in their hands, fully satisfied they would pronounce him not guilty of the dreadful charge against him.

After the prosecution had laid out their reasons for believing the case against Gould had been proven beyond all reasonable doubt, Baron Alderson summed up the evidence and outlined for the jury the choices they had. If they believed the whole of the testimony given by the witnesses, they would find the prisoner guilty. If, however, the facts sworn to could, in their judgement, be accounted for on any other grounds than of the prisoner being a murderer, then they would say so by a verdict of acquittal. Advising them that an awful responsibility lay in their hands in deciding the fate of a fellow-creature, Baron Alderson implored God to direct the jury to a just and righteous verdict.

The trial had begun at 10am and by the time the jury retired to consider their verdict, at 11:30pm, perhaps even God was becoming impatient. It took only a few minutes for the jury to return and deliver their verdict of, 'Not Guilty.'

Even Richard Gould, who had sat composed throughout the entire day, taking copious amounts of notes, did not have the strength to celebrate, as he was quickly led from the dock.

8 CHAPTER EIGHT

Due to concerns over his safety, Gould was not released immediately. The authorities waited until the crowd, which remained entrenched around the Session House for several hours after the trial concluded, had finally dispersed. At around 3pm on the day following the trial, Gould was formally released from Newgate Prison. There was no one waiting to welcome him.

It came to light that, on the eve of his trial, Gould had been formally discharged from the regiment to which he had been attached and from which he had deserted. On the basis that it was the custom of the military authorities not to suffer any person connected to the army and charged with a capital offence to be tried by a criminal tribunal, Gould's discharge had been transmitted from Horse Guards to the Governor of Newgate Prison.

The murder of John Templeman remaining unsolved and it did not take long for the local losers to step forward with their fanciful tales, after the consumption of one too many beers. One such character, forty-year-old Thomas Henry Cornwall, was soon confessing, to the keeper of a beer-shop in Long Lane, that he had been a party to the murder of Mr Templeman.

Cornwall had been drinking in the beer-shop for some time when the general conversation turned to the Islington murder. Emboldened by his alcohol consumption, Cornwall declared he had an intimate knowledge of the murder, then he went further and stated it had, in fact, been him that had held the old man down, whilst Gould had cut his throat. The two, claimed Cornwall, had then split the proceeds of the crime, with Gould taking the lion's share.

Mr Povoss, the man who ran the beer-shop, warned Cornwall it was far too soon to be speaking in such a way about the murder, but Cornwall took no notice and repeated his claims to anyone who was willing to listen. Eventually, Povoss, who had heard the story once too often, stopped a passing policeman and asked Cornwall to repeat what he had said, in front of the officer. When the drunken clown foolishly did so, the policeman took him into custody.

Although nobody believed his story, Cornwall appeared on a charge of disorderly conduct, at Guildhall. When asked what he now had to say about the matter, by Alderman Johnson, Cornwall merely laughed and said, 'Of course I was only joking, I was feeling a little fresh.'

The Alderman was singularly unimpressed and asked Cornwall how he made a living. 'I make some money by singing and giving recitations in public houses,' Cornwall replied. The Alderman decided to relieve him of some of this money and fined Cornwall five shillings.

With the police investigation having stalled, on 6 May 1840 the Home Secretary, Lord Normanby, announced the offer of a reward of £200 and a pardon for anyone who would provide information leading to the apprehension and conviction of the actual murderer of John Templeman. It would have been difficult to have predicted the events that would follow this offer of reward.

Police-Sergeant Charles Otway, of A Division, remained convinced that, despite his acquittal, Gould had been guilty of the murder of John Templeman. Otway decided to do everything in his power, and anything that would be required beyond his power, to bring Gould to justice.

Otway, with the backing of the Commissioner of Police, decided to set a trap to ensnare Gould. Almost everyone held the belief Gould had, at the very least, been involved in the robbery and had information regarding who had murdered Mr Templeman. The police officer made the decision to track down Gould and tempt him with a share of the reward if he was willing to tell everything he knew about the affair.

Sergeant Otway's investigations led him to discover that, following his release from Newgate, Gould had accepted sanctuary, for his own safety, at the Giltspur Street Compter. The Compter was a small prison, generally used to house small-scale debtors, located close to Newgate Prison.

When he arrived at the Compter, Otway was informed Gould was no longer there. The man who had previously declared he considered transportation to be a fate worse than death, had apparently taken the advice of a well-meaning Alderman and was due to set sail from Gravesend, bound for Sydney, Australia, on a free passage, to begin a new life under the name Kelly.

The panic-stricken policeman rushed to Gravesend, on the south bank of the Thames estuary, from where the ship, 'The Elizabeth', was due to convey Gould beyond his reach. Otway arrived just before the ship was due to sail and succeeded in getting on board and locating his quarry.

The breathless policeman informed Gould of the £200 reward on offer, informing him the offer was not due to be made public in the newspapers until the following day. Otway persuaded Gould he'd be foolish not to cash in on any information he held. The clincher in persuading Gould to disembark from the ship, was when Otway convinced him the sharing of information would be entirely risk-free from Gould's perspective, given he could not be tried twice for the same crime.

Safe in the knowledge he was free from the prospect of any further charges in relation to the murder of John Templeman, and having negotiated a £100 upfront share of the reward, Gould provided the following statement:-

'The robbery of Mr Templeman's house was first proposed after he'd been seen showing off his bank-notes. It had been talked over for some time, by Jarvis, his wife and I, but it was not finally agreed upon until the Sunday morning when we decided it would take place on the Monday night. I was at their house but did not stay for long, as Jarvis was expecting a visit from his brother.

Shortly before I left, Jarvis went into the garden and got a piece of wood, which he used as a dibber. He bored a hole in the handle and passed a piece of string through it, to hang it on his arm.

I then went to the Flora Tavern, in York Place, and got drunk. Later, I went back to my lodgings and went to bed. I was meant to have gone to the Jarvis's on the following morning, but I'd lain in bed for so long that Mrs Jarvis had to come and get me. Jarvis had given her a message regarding how the robbery was to be done.

I was told not to go near the place until after the public-houses were closed. Mrs Jarvis told me she'd prepared breakfast and there was no fear of me being noticed, so I went there first, then I went to the Rainbow Public House and remained there, until twelve o'clock at night. At that hour, I went to Jarvis's house and from there we went together to Mr Templeman's.

Mrs Jarvis was stationed at the door of her own cottage and was told to give us a warning if anyone came by. I removed a piece of paper that was pasted over one of the windows and then pushed my hand through the gap to reach the little button inside. I climbed through the opened window and Jarvis followed me. I broke open a box, which was in the sitting-room, and found some silver. Jarvis went into the bedroom.

Jarvis came back and suggested that, as the notes had not been found, they must have been under the old man's head. Jarvis said we would have to keep Mr Templeman quiet and tie him up, we'd brought a cord with us for that purpose. Jarvis struck the old man with the dibber when he jumped out of bed to try and resist. After several more blows, the old man was overpowered and his hands were tied. Jarvis tied stockings, that he'd found lying nearby, over the man's eyes.

We continued to search for the notes and eventually found them in a drawer in the box in which I'd found the silver. On closer inspection, we found the notes were useless, they were to be drawn upon 'The Bank of Fashion'.

At this time, the old man called out, 'I know you!' Jarvis then told me he would rather finish the old man off than be found out and he went into the bedroom on his own. I climbed back out of the house, through the window, and Jarvis followed soon afterwards.

We then went back to Jarvis's house. I proposed we divide up the money, but Jarvis said, 'No, we'd better hide it because the cottages here will all be searched?' I took the dibber away and threw it into the New River, then I threw the dark lantern which we'd used, into a pond in Pocock's Fields.

Later, I went up by the Angel and went to a coffee-stall, by the corner of the New Road, where I had some coffee and stopped for about half an hour. There was a man there, selling some pictures to a young woman. He sold one for four shillings and sixpence. I asked if there was a tobacco shop open and the man said he didn't know. I then asked him to sell me a pipe, before I headed home.

When I returned home, it was two o'clock. I went to bed and the following morning placed all the money, except nine shillings, in an old stocking, which I then hid it in the privy. The stocking was an odd one, belonging to myself.

I'd agreed to meet Mrs Jarvis the next morning, at the Three Goat's Heads, Wandsworth Road. After she arrived with her child, we had a pint and a half of beer and a quart of gin. On the way back, we went to Lambeth Walk and I bought a pair of boots for seven and sixpence and paid for them with the silver. When we came out, I proposed to throw the old ones away, as they were not worth anything, but she said, 'Don't do that, Dick, I'll go and sell them. Even if they only fetch a quarter, it's better than nothing.' She went and sold them for tuppence in Oakley Street, Lambeth.

I asked Mrs Jarvis if she'd said anything to the neighbour's girl, Thornton, in the morning, when she'd seen her. She said no. She said she'd seen a man called Ellis come along and she had told him she was going to her sister's house for screws. I told her that, since she had said it, she'd better go there. She could then give an account of herself if she came under suspicion. She went and I waited at the General Wolf, Grey's Inn Lane.

We then met and went to the Belvedere, Pentonville, and she got a quarter of gin on trust. We then went to Thornhill Hill Road, where we bumped into Ellis. After speaking to him, I went to the Rainbow and she went home. I agreed to go to her house for tea, but, when it came to dusk, she arrived at the Rainbow and told me there was a rare stink about the murder and I'd better stay away that night.

I went home and was apprehended at 11:30pm that night.'

The following morning, rather than receiving his promised £100 share of the reward money, Gould was rendered dumbstruck, as he was told by Police-Sergeant Charles Otway that he was under arrest for the robbery of Mr John Templeman.

Gould was conveyed to London by steam-boat and was brought before the Chief Magistrate, Mr Hall, at Bow Street Police Court, on 11 May 1840.

As a familiar list of characters was called upon to testify against him once again, Gould said to Mr Hall, 'I wish to know if there is anything fresh to be brought against me because all these witnesses have already been examined at my trial. I was tried and acquitted of the charge brought against me and therefore, unless there are fresh facts, I cannot see why I should be placed here.'

'You are not going to be tried for the same offence,' Hall said. 'The present Inquiry relates to the property of the deceased and not to his murder. For that offence, you have already been tried and acquitted.' Gould was then remanded pending further investigation.

During his next appearance before Mr Hall, the confession Gould had provided to Sergeant Otway was read out. Having heard the confession, Hall said, 'It is quite clear this man is not entitled to the reward, because, by his own statement, it is clear he has not only been a party to the robbery, but also to the murder.'

There then followed a three-way discussion between Hall, Sergeant Otway and Gould over what exactly the policeman had offered to Gould. Otway made it clear he had never said to the prisoner he could not be tried for robbery and Gould was once again remanded.

John and Mary Jarvis were then brought forward. The couple's child was now back in the arms of Mrs Jarvis, though their frosty relationship did not appear to have thawed any and a policeman was placed between them in the dock.

Hall asked if any evidence was to be presented against the two prisoners and was informed there would be none whatsoever. He then asked John Jarvis if he still worked at the same place of employment as before and was told by Jarvis that he'd been discharged the previous Saturday, but had since gained employment elsewhere.

The magistrate ordered the couple to be discharged, on the promise they would come forward at any time their presence may be required. After they were led from the bar, the unhappily married couple did not acknowledge each other and went their separate ways.

As police officers struggled to ensure that only witnesses were allowed entry to the already packed-out Bow Street Police Court, the examination of Richard Gould, on the charge of burglary, resumed on 13 May 1840.

Mr Hobler appeared for the prosecution and Gould, having lost all faith in the justice system, represented himself. On entering the room, Mr Hall introduced the Duke of Brunswick and his equerry, Baron Aulan, both of whom would stay to witness the day's proceedings.

Hobler began by stating he intended to call witnesses who would provide evidence showing that, on the day prior to the murder, the deceased, Mr Templeman, received some money, and that the prisoner was in possession of similar money when he was apprehended. It would, however, the prosecutor claimed, be necessary for time to be afforded to procure additional evidence and so he asked for the prisoner to be remanded again at the end of the day's proceedings, in order that the purposes of justice might be answered.

Witnesses were then called to testify to the various funds Templeman had collected on the eve of his murder.

When Hannah Morgan provided her testimony, Gould asked her, 'Was there not some marked money among that which you gave him?'

'No, there was not,' Morgan replied.

'Did you not say, in previous statements you have provided, that there was?'

'I did say there was a marked shilling amongst the money, but I was wrong, I found that shilling afterwards.'

Gould turned to Mr Hall, saying, 'I don't feel it is right, your worship, that the witness should be allowed to change her testimony.'

'The witness has merely corrected her former statement regarding the marked shilling, there is nothing wrong in that,' Hall replied.

The next witness, Robert King, provided a statement regarding Gould's appearance at the Rainbow Public House on the night before the robbery, of Gould's lack of funds and the game of skittles that was played. King's statement managed to rile Gould.

'Before we played a game of skittles for a half-ounce of tobacco, had I not played you for some beer?' Gould asked.

'I don't think you did,' King replied.

'Now think hard,' Gould pressed, 'did I not play you for a pot of beer?'

'I have no recollection of it.'

Gould had no intention of letting the matter rest. 'I have asked you a plain and simple question and I expect a plain answer. Will you swear, positively, I did not play you for a pot of beer?'

'To the best of my knowledge, you did not,' King mumbled.

'That is no answer,' Gould snapped, 'were you drunk at the time?'

'I can't say I was downright sober.'

'So, you were drunk. Now, have you not been talking this matter over since you heard of the murder?'

'No, I never talked about it at all.'

'That seems highly unlikely,' Gould sneered, 'but I shall be able to prove I paid for beer and other things that night.'

Mr Hobler asked the witness how drunk he'd been on the night in question and King responded, 'Not so drunk that I did not know what I was about.'

The next witness, Robert Pizey, swore as to Gould having given him money to purchase a rushlight on his behalf.

Pizey's evidence was followed by that of Police-Constable John Collins, who began by providing a statement regarding his search of Mr Templeman's cottage. He was then asked by Hobler, 'In consequence of some further information you lately received, did you carry out any further search around Pocock's Fields.'

'Yes, I did,' the policeman replied. 'I went yesterday and made a search in a large pond in Pocock's Fields that runs into a common sewer. Having caused the pond to be emptied of the water it contained, I found a dark lantern, which I now produce, with a piece of rushlight in it. It was found in the mud at the bottom of the pond.'

Mr Hall asked the witness, 'Were you present when the prisoner was examined here on Monday last?'

'I was,' Collins replied.

'Did you hear Sergeant Otway give evidence regarding a statement made to him by the prisoner?'

'I heard that statement and, in consequence of it, I searched the pond in question.'

'Where is this pond situated, with reference to Allen's cottage and that of the deceased?' Hall asked.

'It lies between the two, about twenty yards from Allen's cottage and not very far from the other,' the constable replied.

The Magistrate then turned to Gould. 'Do you have any questions you wish to put to this witness?' he asked.

'I have only one question to ask him,' the prisoner replied, as the colour visibly drained from his face. 'Had you not searched this pond previously, when you were carrying out a search of the area around Pocock's Field?'

'I found the lantern in the pond at 3:30pm on Tuesday the thirteenth. I did not go to look for it before then and no other officer had searched the pond previously,' Collins replied.

A procession of familiar witness appeared, before Mrs Mary Allen provided her testimony regarding her former lodger. After her statement, Gould had several questions for the witness.

'You say that when I got up on the Tuesday morning, I went to the wash-house and then to the water-closet. Was there anything unusual about that?'

'No, there was not,' Mrs Allen replied.

'Was I not in the habit of doing so every morning?'

'Yes, you certainly were.'

'Is there not a door leading from the water-closet into your garden?'

'Yes, there is.'

'And could not any person passing through the garden get into the water-closet?' Gould asked.

'Yes, but not into the wash-house, unless I opened the door,' Mrs Allen replied.

'Were not persons in the habit of passing through the garden as a shortcut?'

'The neighbours may have done so occasionally, but strangers would have been warned off and prevented.'

'You say you found a pair of odd stockings rolled up on the box beside my bed. How do you know they were odd stockings if they were rolled up?'

'I knew there was more than one stocking from the size and feel.'

'Yes, but how did you know they were odd and how were you able to identify one of them as being the one in which the money was later discovered? Was there any particular marking on the stocking that would allow you to swear so positively to it?'

'There was no mark upon it, as far as I am aware, but I believe it to be the same stocking.'

'But you will not undertake to swear it is the same stocking?'

'I swear it to the best of my belief.'

'Are there not thousands of stockings exactly like it? Come now, answer that, and get to the point. Why are you trying to injure me?' Gould pleaded.

'It is not my wish to injure you Richard, but I'm sworn to tell the truth,' Mrs Allen replied.

'You said your husband and you noticed my new shoes after I came into the house. Was there anything between us at the time?'

'Yes, certainly, the table was between us at the time.'

'Do you mean to say that you could see through the table?'

'No. When I first noticed the new shoes, you were sitting by the fire.'

'On another point, was I not frequently in the habit of staying out late and have I not sometimes remained out all night?'

'Not since you were out of a situation. I'd never known you to stop out all night, except on one occasion.'

With that, Mrs Allen stepped down and Mr Hobler informed the Magistrate he had no further evidence to present at that time. He asked for Gould to be remanded until the following Tuesday.

An irate Gould said he could see no possible reason why he should be remanded for so long a time. The evidence had all been brought up before, Gould claimed, and he was at a loss to see why it should take so long to produce it again.

Hobler explained he had no access to any former evidence and even if he had, he could not use it, as this was a different charge. The lawyer said he had no wish to press with unnecessary severity against the prisoner, but claimed there was still a mass of evidence to be brought forward, which would take considerable time to arrange.

The Magistrate placed Gould upon remand until the following Tuesday.

Proceedings resumed on 19 May, beginning with a familiar statement from Charles Allen, before Hobler focused on a missing dark lantern.

'Do you remember having seen a dark lantern in your house at any time?' Hobler asked.

'Yes, I had a dark lantern,' Charles Allen replied. 'I swear it is the one that has been produced in Court.

My father and I have had it in our possession for the last forty years.'

'When did you last see it?' the lawyer asked.

'I cannot say exactly when I saw it last, it was kept either in a box or a cupboard. The horn was out of it when I saw it last and I'm sure it is the same one because the horn is a little burst. The prisoner could have had access to the lantern at any time whilst he was lodging in my house.'

'Do you see a piece of rushlight in the lantern?'

'Yes, I do.'

'Did you place it there?'

'No, I did not. I do not think I could have seen the lantern for a year and a half before the murder took place. I never use a rushlight in my house.'

Mr Hall turned to Gould and asked if he had any questions he wished to put to the witness. Nodding, Gould faced Allen and asked, 'With respect to this lantern, you say you have not seen it for a year and a half. Was it not always kept in the cupboard, over the place where the coals are kept, and might not any person have seen it there?'

'Of course, it could be seen if it had been there,' Allen replied.

'Was not that cupboard always kept open?' Gould asked.

'One side of it was generally open, there was no lock to it.'

'Now, have you not frequently missed articles from your house?'

'I have sometimes missed things that the neighbour's boys have taken away, but I have generally found them.'

'What distance is your cottage from this pond in which the lantern was found?'

'About thirty yards.'

'Is there a fence or enclosure between your cottage and the pond?'

'No, there was none at the time, although there is now,' Allen replied.

'Did not little boys used to play around the pond?' Gould asked.

'Yes, they did.'

'You say you kept no rushlight in your house. Is it not true that I often used to stay up late at night to read?'

'No, not to my knowledge Richard.'

'Do you mean to say you never knew me to burn a light in my bedroom?' Gould asked, an astonished look forming on his face.

'You never burned a light in your room to my knowledge.'

'Let me just ask you one more question Mr Allen,' Gould said. 'With respect to the money I had on the Tuesday night, did I not say I had been lucky and the old lady, meaning my aunt, had received me kindly? How is it you have omitted to state that fact now, given you have mentioned it on other occasions?'

'I might have said what you remind me of,' Allen spluttered, 'and I now remember you did say something about your aunt receiving you kindly.'

'You have been examined about this business several times now Mr Allen and I am rather surprised you should not have recollected about the money before now,' Gould sneered, before the witness was excused.

The next witness to be called was Police-Sergeant Thomas King. After describing his initial search of Allen's cottage and the discovery of the money-filled stocking, King was asked by Mr Hobler if he had carried out any subsequent searches.

'Yes,' the policeman replied. 'On Thursday last, I went back to Allen's cottage with four constables. We searched the same pond in which the lantern was found and, while I was searching, I saw something stuck in the mud and told one of the constables to see what it was. He did so and pulled a chisel from the mud, which I now produce for the Court.'

'I have seen the chest of drawers in Mr Templeman's house,' King continued, 'and there are marks of violence on one of the drawers, that which I produce today. The marks appear to have been made recently and seem to correspond with the chisel.'

'Did you discover anything else during your search of this pond?' Gould asked.

'I found a great many things in the pond, pint pots and items of no real value.'

The next policeman to be called was Police Sergeant Richard Bradshaw, who stated, 'On Monday 11 May, I brought the prisoner, in a cab, from the House of Correction, Clerkenwell, to this Court. On our way, the prisoner asked if we were going to Bow Street. I said we were and he asked if he was going to give evidence. I told him he was going to be examined and he said I must be mistaken, as he had already been tried for the murder. I told him he was not being tried for the murder, but for the robbery. He said he had been told by Sergeant Otway that he was to be set free and I told him I knew nothing about that. He then leant back in the cab and said, 'Oh well, I don't care, they can't top me for that.''

George Hoare, the head turnkey at Coldbath Fields Prison, was heard next. 'The prisoner was brought into the prison on the evening of 9 May, at about 6:15pm. He told me he wished to make a statement regarding the murder of Mr Templeman and said he wished to disclose the names of the parties involved. He claimed he himself had suffered enough already and said he felt entitled to the £200 reward on offer. I said I knew nothing about the reward, but I took down his statement in writing and it was then signed by us both and formally witnessed by the Governor.'

The confession was read, in full, to the Court by the Chief Clerk. It was, in substance, largely the same as the one Gould would later provide to Sergeant Otway, naming John Jarvis as the principal party in the murder.

With no further evidence being offered, Mr Hall addressed Gould. 'You may now, if you please, address any observations you may have to the bench. You should note, however, that anything you say will be taken down in writing and may be used against you. I should, perhaps, remind you that you have already made a statement, the whole of which you have subsequently declared to be false.'

Gould decided to roll the dice and speak up. 'Your worship, as to the evidence, I know it would be worthless for me to say anything about it at present. I think it right, however, to be fair to persons I have alluded to in my statement, to say under what circumstances I made it.'

'Sergeant Otway came to me at Gravesend,' Gould continued, 'and said he had been directed, by the

Secretary of State, to inform me that a reward of £200 was about to be offered for information leading to the capture of the murderer of John Templeman. Otway said it was the wish of the Secretary of State that the matter was mentioned to me before the offer of a reward was made public.'

'At that time,' Gould claimed, 'I was not aware that Otway was a police officer. I told him I did not want to make any statement on the matter. He then began to reason with me, saying how serviceable a sum it would be to me, as I was leaving the country. I maintained my position, stating that I had no information to provide and that I would have nothing at all to do with the matter. In the event of there not being a conviction, I would have lost my passage and would have been worse off than before.'

'Otway then asked me, if he were to bring me £100 and lay it in front of me, would I tell him who the actual guilty parties were, bearing in mind I could not be tried again. I told him that, for a guaranteed £100, I would tell him who the actual parties were. He put my statement into writing, then left. When he returned the following day, he took me into custody.'

'As we were coming from Gravesend,' Gould said, 'I asked him how it was that he had apprehended me without a warrant. He said that, as matters stood, I could be tried for robbery and, likewise, if I knew the parties concerned, I could be punished for that also. Having stated what I had, I found myself in a very awkward position. After I was charged with robbery and brought to this place, I made up my mind to make up some sort of statement that would best coincide with the evidence, which I according did. After I had done so, I felt I was acting very wrongly and I took the opportunity, after my first appearance here, to contradict my statement.'

'Have you anything more to say?' the Magistrate asked.

'Only this,' Gould replied, 'that I made a statement under the impression I could not be charged again. As I supposed I was leaving the country, it was a matter of very little difference to me whether people thought I committed the murder. I was only interested in getting the £100 and it was my intention, once I had got the money, to say I had committed the murder myself, it being my belief I could not be tried again.'

Hall asked Gould if he would sign the declaration he had just made and the prisoner duly agreed to do so.

After the statement had been signed, Hall directed Sergeant Otway to stand forward. The Magistrate then asked the policeman, 'Did you, at any time, urge the prisoner, or offer him any inducement, to sign the original statement he provided you with?'

'I did not, your worship,' Otway replied.

The magistrate then formally committed Richard Gould to be tried at the Central Criminal Court, on the charge of the robbery of John Templeman.

9 CHAPTER NINE

Richard Gould appeared before Baron James Parke and Lord Chief Justice Tindal, at the Central Criminal Court, on 15 June 1840. Messrs Bodkin and Ballantyne conducted the prosecution, Gould again decided he would be best served by representing himself.

As high profile as the case had been, on this particular day it took second billing to the trial of another potman, Mr Edward Oxford, who stood on a charge of high treason, having attempted to assassinate the Queen. It was only after an agreement was reached to postpone the Edward Oxford trial, that Gould was placed in the dock.

As we have already covered, in some detail, the evidence provided by the witnesses at the previous Inquests, Inquiries and Court sessions, in this section we will concentrate on the questions put to the witnesses by the prosecutors and Gould.

Questioning of Mary Thornton:-

Gould: 'You were often in the habit of being with Mr Templeman and cleaning in his house were you not?'

Mary Thornton: 'Yes.'

Gould: 'Have you ever seen me converse with the deceased?'

Mary Thornton: 'I have seen you serve him with beer, while you were at the Castle Public House. I cannot say how long ago that was. I have seen you stop to converse with Mr Templeman.'

Gould: 'When was the last time you saw the window that was allegedly broken to gain entry to the cottage?'

Mary Thornton: 'The last time I saw the window, was the Sunday before the murder.'

Questioning of Francis Capriani:-

Gould: 'How long had you been carrying out work for Mr Templeman?'

Capriani: 'I was at work for him for about a fortnight or three weeks before his death. I finished work on the piece of ground on Monday, the 16th of March.'

Gould: 'Did you ever, while you were at work on that ground, see me in, at, or near Mr Templeman's or Jarvis's cottages?'

Capriani: 'Not that day. I did not see you. I've never noticed you in the garden.'

Gould: 'Could I have passed without you seeing me?'

Capriani: 'You could have got there without passing me, but not on the ordinary path. I should not think you could have passed without my seeing you when I was working in the garden.'

Questioning of Jane Lovett:-

Gould: 'What could have occasioned you to have noticed so particularly the coins you paid to Mr Templeman?'

Lovett: 'Because I counted the money out into his hands.'

Gould: 'Were any of the coins marked?'

Lovett: 'No, none were marked, to my knowledge.'

Gould: 'Have you ever said they were?'

Lovett: 'I have said no more than that I had a marked shilling in my possession, but whether I gave it him or not, I cannot say.'

Mr Bodkin: 'Have you, since you said that, looked for that marked shilling?'

Lovett: 'Yes, I found it in my possession when I got home and therefore I did not give it to Mr Templeman.'

Questioning of Henry Wright:-

Gould: 'How long had you lodged with me at Allen's?'

Wright: 'Five or six months. You did not lodge there the whole time with me, you were away for a fortnight, or it might have been longer.'

Gould: 'In that time, have you ever known me to be out for any improper purpose?'

Wright: 'During that six months, I never knew you to be out for any improper purpose. I have known you to be out till past twelve or one o'clock. I cannot say I have known what you have been doing, perhaps you have been after a situation and stopped at public houses.'

Gould: 'Have you ever seen a dark lantern in Allen's cottage?'

Wright: 'I never saw a lantern lying about in Allen's cottage during the six months I was there.'

Gould: 'What is the informal arrangement between potmen, when one or the other is short of money?'

Wright: 'It is the custom between potmen to treat one another when out of place.'

Gould: 'Now, suppose I had come to you and said, 'I have 5d or 6d in my pocket, I do not know how soon I shall need it, will you treat me with some beer?' Would you have given it to me, or expected me to pay for it?'

Wright: 'I would have given it to you.'

Gould: 'Is it true I was generally in the habit of collecting my debts on a Sunday morning, while you lodged with me?'

Wright: 'Yes, you used to go out to collect whatever debt there was. You have, in the past, told me you had four or five shillings owing to you at the cottages.'

Gould: 'On your oath, sir, how many times have you been in custody?'

Wright: 'I have never been in custody for a felony. I was in custody, but never convicted, on suspicion of stealing a cash-box.'

Gould: 'You have said you had some conversation with Richard Squires, what was it about?'

Wright: 'When I saw Squires, I asked him if you had said anything to him. He said, 'No.' I told him what you had said to me, that you had been talking about committing a robbery. I did not tell Squires all that passed between you and me. I told him what you had said about intending to commit a robbery on an old man.'

Bodkin: 'How long is it since you left the Duchess of Kent Public House?'

Wright: 'Four weeks. Since then I have been attending at Bow Street and other places, regarding this trial.'

Bodkin: 'Were you ever tried for stealing a cash-box?'

Wright: 'I was not tried for stealing the cash-box. I was taken to Hatton Garden and had a hearing. The Magistrate discharged me and the person in whose service I had lived for nine years took me on again.'

Questioning of John Richard Jobson:-

Gould: 'Now, Mr Jobson, what work is it in which you allude to having seen the words 'darkey' and 'screw'?'

Jobson: 'Tom and Jerry'. I have seen it in two works. I have seen it in ………'

Gould (interrupting): 'Have you not stated it was in 'Bell's Life in London' that you saw them?'

Jobson: 'I did say so, but that was a mistake.'

Gould: 'Now, Mr Jobson, please be good enough to tell the Court how many times you have been in custody?'

Jobson: 'I have been twice in custody, once for being drunk and disorderly and once for being in company with a drunken man, who gave me into custody for robbing him of a shilling. You were in my company then and offered the man five shillings to abandon the charge. After that, the man wanted the policeman to let me go, but the policeman said it was too late, as the charge had already been booked.'

Bodkin: 'So, because the charge of stealing a shilling was entered on the sheet, you could not be liberated?'

Jobson: 'Yes. I went in the morning to Worship Street and was discharged without witnesses being called.'

Gould: 'How would you speak as to my character at that time?'

Jobson: 'I should say your character was equally as good as mine, only you were a deserter at the time.'

Gould: 'By what means do you make a living?'

Jobson: 'I colour caricatures, or anything I can, to get my living. I have done some hundreds or thousands of religious prints, but, through seeing you, I have now not got even one to colour, my work has been stopped.'

Gould: 'Do you not buy and sell goods?'

Jobson: 'I am not in the habit of dealing. I have been to fairs and races for pleasure, but I never buy things there and bring them to London.'

Questioning of James (Jem) Rogers:-

Gould: 'Before you came to give any evidence against me, had not you had some conversation with Jobson?'

Rogers: 'No.'

Gould: 'What was it that induced you to come forward and give evidence?'

Rogers: 'I, now and then, read the newspaper, but very seldom. If I heard anything from the newspaper, it used to be more told to me than me reading it myself. It was in consequence of what I saw in the newspaper that I came to give evidence. It was stated in the newspaper that I was not yet in custody and I thought that not having committed any crime, the best way to clear myself would be to make an appearance.'

Gould: 'So, that was the cause of your making up this tale?'

Rogers: 'I believe it is the truth I have stated.'

Gould: 'What do you know of 'screws' and 'darkeys'?'

Rogers: 'I had heard the phrase 'screws' before, as meaning skeleton keys and 'darkeys' as meaning a dark-lantern.'

Gould: 'Do umbrella-makers generally keep such things?'

Rogers: 'No, but I formerly kept an old-iron shop and I suppose you thought I might still have such things.'

Gould: 'Did I make any offer to you to purchase these items?'

Rogers: 'You did not want to purchase them, but to borrow them.'

Gould: 'When I spoke to you about the 'screws' and 'darkey', did you think I was joking, or in earnest?'

Rogers: 'I could not say whether you were serious or joking. I passed it off as a joke, but I cannot say what your intention was.'

Gould: 'If you had not seen your name mentioned in the newspaper, would you have thought of coming to give evidence?'

Rogers: 'You are the last person in the world I should have come against, or thought of coming against or seeing in the situation in which you are placed. I said I was sorry to see you as you were because you seemed to be so poor and when you were working in the public-house you always had a shilling in your pocket. You told me you had no money. I believe you said so after I said I was sorry to see you as you were, but I cannot be positive.'

Bodkin: 'What was the prisoner's general appearance at the time of your conversation?'

Rogers: 'He was generally dressed in a plush waistcoat, but he was not dressed as well as I had formerly seen him.'

Questioning of Robert Pizey:-

Gould: 'How far from the Rainbow is the shop where you bought the rushlight?'

Pizey: 'I should say forty yards, not more, it was on Felix Terrace.'

Gould: 'Did I make any secret of asking you to fetch me a rushlight? Did I ask you to hide it from the others in the room?'

Pizey: 'You did not make any secret of it. I brought it back into the tap-room and gave it to you in front of the others in the room.'

Gould: 'Don't you think, if I meant it for any secret purpose, I should have fetched it myself?'

Pizey: 'I do not know. You are not the first man for whom I have fetched a candle.'

Questioning of Robert King:-

Gould: 'After we left the house, how long did we stay talking outside the door?'

King: 'A very few minutes, not five minutes, we were not together five minutes after we came out of the house. You then went up towards the workhouse, up by Laycock's, towards Park Street.'

Judge: 'Did he go away by himself?'

King: 'Yes. He crossed over from the Rainbow, on the workhouse side. We bid one another good night and parted. He then crossed to the workhouse and I had to turn right to go down my street. No one was with him when he parted from me. He went towards Allen's cottage, where he was living. He went the way that would lead there.'

Gould: 'Did you see anything unusual in my manner?'

King: 'No.'

Gould: 'Was I carrying anything that would have raised any suspicion?'

King: 'I did not see anything in your possession at all.'

Ballantyne: 'Do you know Mr Templeman's house?'

King: 'Yes, he went in that direction, it is near Allen's.'

Questioning of Mary King:-

Gould: 'How long were you at the Rainbow?'

Mary King: 'About a quarter of an hour, it was twenty minutes to twelve when we came out.'

Gould: 'What exactly is it you claim to have seen in my pocket?'

Mary King: 'The thing in your pocket was long and appeared to be bundled up in one corner of your pocket.'

Gould: 'When did you supposedly see this item?'

Mary King: 'While I was in the Rainbow.'

Gould: 'Where were you seated and where was I?'

Mary King: 'I was against the door, I was in company with someone. The room is divided into boxes. You were sitting beside the fireplace.'

Gould: 'Have you the audacity to swear you could see, in those few minutes, from one box to the other, what I had in my pocket?'

Mary King: 'When you got up and turned yourself towards the fire-place, that was when I saw it. I have never said I saw it sticking out of your pocket, I saw something in your pocket.'

Judge: 'Could you form any judgment regarding what this was in his pocket?'

Mary King: 'As well as I could see, it was a piece of wood or something like that.'

Bodkin: 'About what was the size of what you thought was the bundle?'

Mary King: 'It was round. It was larger than that inkstand, or about the size of that bottle. I did not actually see any part of it or anything that would confirm it was a piece of wood. I should say it was about a foot long.'

Questioning of Charles Allen:-

Gould: 'Have you ever said it was two years since you saw the missing lantern?'

Allen: 'I never swore so, I do not recollect saying so.'

Gould: 'When do you claim to have last used the lantern?'

Allen: 'I had it to go and look at the sow. The pigsty and the house are all attached together, it is all one brick wall, but you must go out of the house to go to the pigsty.'

Gould: 'Where did you put the lantern, after you had finished using it?'

Allen: 'After I used the lantern, I placed it in the cupboard. I am confident I put it there, but, after using it for the pigs, I used it in the wash-house and, during that week, I used it four or five times. My wife then put it either in the cupboard or the box, she can speak more clearly as to where it was.'

Gould: 'Have you not been often troubled by persons crossing your garden, both after you have been in bed and in the daytime?'

Allen: 'Sometimes people have gone across my garden and I have noticed it, but I was not troubled with anybody because I did not see them. I have had occasion to go out to stop them from crossing the garden, but I do not term that trouble, I only did it as a friendly action.'

Gould: 'Have you not had trouble with the neighbour's children removing things from the garden?'

Allen: 'I have not been frequently robbed of little things by my neighbour's children. I have lost things twice since I have been there, but I always found them.'

Gould: 'Do you recognise the lantern produced in Court as being the one owned by you?'

Allen: 'I have used the lantern so often I can almost swear it is my father's lantern.'

Bodkin: 'Since that lantern has been found, have you looked for your own?'

Allen: 'Yes, everywhere, and I can find no trace of it.'

Questioning of Mary Allen:-

Gould: 'Was my bedroom window fastened when your husband locked the door upon me?'

Mary Allen: 'No, there was no fastening to your bedroom window, only a pulley.'

Gould: 'Could any person get out of that window?'

Mary Allen: 'I could not have got out of it myself, not without considerable difficulty.'

Gould: 'Do you not think I could have escaped by means of that window, had I pleased?'

Mary Allen: 'I do not know whether you could have got out of it. I do not know how high the window is from the ground. You can stand in the room and look out of it. You cannot reach the top of the window, you can reach to the centre.'

Gould: 'Can you recall what happened to the lantern after your husband had used it?'

Mary Allen: 'I remember taking the lantern off the table and putting it away after my husband had used it?'

Gould: 'Would anyone have had access to the cupboard in which the lantern was kept?'

Mary Allen: 'We have never had anyone but you and Wright lodging in our house since we had the lantern. I cannot say whether you were in the habit of going into my boxes or cupboards. You were often in the house, you could go to them if you liked.'

Gould: 'You have sworn the stocking produced in Court is like the stockings you saw on the box. Is there any mark on it which causes you to think so?'

Mary Allen: 'I know the stockings by their general appearance.'

Gould: 'General appearance is not evidence. I ask you again, Mrs Allen, by what mark or proof do you know these stockings to be mine?'

Mary Allen: 'It is exactly the same kind of stocking, here is the mark around the top. I looked at them when I found them in your room. When the police discovered the stocking the next morning, I saw it was exactly the same stocking?'

Gould: 'Have you ever mended stockings for me?'

Mary Allen: 'I have footed stockings for you when I washed for you. I have no recollection whatever of mending this one. You had two pairs when I washed for you a month before Christmas and I had mended them for you.'

Gould: 'Do you suppose two pairs of white cotton stockings, in constant use, would last me that length of time and be as good as these?'

Mary Allen: 'I can't say whether you wore them all the time, or not. I know nothing about your replacing those stockings.'

Gould: 'Was it not the custom for me, all the time I lodged with you, to go regularly every Sunday morning to collect what money I had due to me by weekly instalments?'

Mary Allen: 'Not since you left the Barnsbury Castle. You owed me about £1 or £2, but I have never cast it up.'

Gould: 'Now tell the truth, if you had known I had money in my possession, would you not have thought me unprincipled not to pay you?'

Mary Allen: 'You have had money before and offered to pay me and I have said, 'If you are short, you had better let it alone.' I have said so in many instances and I never expected you would pay me, being out of employment.'

Gould: 'How could I be without money, when I offered it you?'

Mary Allen: 'You have had a shilling or so and said, 'I will pay for my tea,' and I have said, 'Never mind.' I knew you were in distress and did not wish to trouble you.'

Gould: 'Have you ever known me to be out for improper motives, or anything unlawful'

Mary Allen: 'I do not know what you were out for. I am not obliged to give you a character reference, I know nothing of your conduct outside of my house.'

Bodkin: 'Have you ever had any quarrel or difference with the prisoner?'

Mary Allen: 'Never in my life.'

Questioning of Police-Constable William Kerr:-

Gould: 'Was Mr Templeman's cottage situated within your beat?'

Kerr: 'No, this was not my beat at that time. Middleton, No. 235, was on that beat that morning, he came on at nine o'clock. Peacock had been on at nine the night before and off at six. The man before him came on at six and went off at nine. Neither of those officers is here.'

Gould: 'From what you saw at the scene, how many persons do you think had been engaged in the murder and robbery of Mr Templeman?'

Kerr: 'I cannot tell. I think one strong man might do it himself, the victim being a feeble old man.'

Gould: 'Have you not previously stated that there must have been two people or more involved?'

Kerr: 'I have never said I was certain there were two or more, I was never asked the question.'

Questioning of Police-Sergeant John Collins:-

Gould: 'Do you recollect accompanying Sergeant Bradshaw to Coldbath Fields, on the 11th of May, to fetch me from the police-office?'

Collins: 'I do.'

Gould: 'Do you recall a conversation that took place regarding carrying out a search for a piece of wood, in consequence of a statement I had given?'

Collins: 'I do not recollect any conversation taking place about searching for some wood in consequence of your statement. I never said a word to you about anything of the sort. I am not aware that Sergeant King or anyone else went on Sunday to search. I said nothing about the statement you had made on Saturday night. You and Bradshaw had some conversation together, but I did not hear it. Nothing was said about any pond then. We were all in a cab and from the rumbling of the cab upon the stones, I could not hear what you said.'

Questioning of Inspector James Miller:-

Gould: 'What was it that led you to carry out a search of the pond at Pocock's Fields?'

Miller: 'I did not myself search the pond in Pocock's Fields. I ordered it to be searched in consequence of a communication I heard made by Otway in your presence. Otway said you had stated that you'd thrown a lantern away into a pond in Pocock's Fields.'

Gould: 'Where was this communication made?'

Miller: 'At Bow Street Police Court, on Monday, the 11th of May.'

Questioning of Police Sergeant George Otway:-

Gould: 'How long had you known I was at the Compter, before your coming to Gravesend?'

Otway: 'Not more than three or four hours.'

Gould: 'What took place during our first meeting at Gravesend?'

Otway: 'I first visited you there at eleven o'clock at night. I represented myself to be an officer. I was dressed in plain clothes. I had no Macintosh on my arm. I left you after about half an hour. I said I had come with the desire to show you a copy of the letter from the Secretary of State. You asked me to show you the letter, then you read the letter twice, I believe. After reading it, you put the letter to one side and said you had made up your mind you would have nothing to do with it. You did not say you knew nothing about it. The paper offered a £200 reward for the discovery of the parties who committed the murder of the late Mr Templeman. You asked me to show you the letter again. I did so, then you said, 'I will have nothing to do with it, but I will tell you what I will do. If they will give me £100, I will tell who the parties were?' I then asked you who the actual parties were that committed the murder and you said, 'Shall I be required to remain in England?' I said that you would and you then said, 'I will tell who the parties are that actually committed the murder if you will give me £100 and pay my passage-money.' That was about ten minutes or a quarter of an hour after I had been with you, it might have been twenty minutes.'

Gould: 'On your oath, did you not persuade me, as I had seen so much trouble through this affair, to make something from it now I had the opportunity?'

Otway: 'Certainly not. I did not tell you how serviceable the money would be to you, as you were about to leave the country. I did not ask you to come to town. I said I should not ask you any questions.'

Gould: 'Do you pretend to swear that, for a quarter of an hour, nothing was said after I refused to have anything to do with the matter for the £200?'

Otway: 'For the greater part of the time, you were leaning your head on your arms, thinking.'

Gould: 'What happened after our conversation?'

Otway: 'In consequence of what you said, I made a report to the Commissioners of Police.'

Gould: 'The following day you came and took me to London. Do you recall the conversation that took place between us on the journey?'

Otway: 'You asked me whether you could be tried again for the murder and I told you no, but you could be tried for the robbery. I did not say you could be punished if you did not make a disclosure, as you had said you knew who the parties were. Scarcely anything further passed on the subject on the way to London.'

Gould: 'And what happened upon our arrival in London?'

Otway: 'I handed you into the custody of Inspector Miller at the station-house. I do not recollect that you made any remark at that time. After you had been placed at the bar at Bow Street and charged with robbery, I accompanied Inspector Miller to the lock-up place to see you. I was not there by myself for but a moment, I went in and came out with Inspector Miller. You asked me whether I was disengaged the next day and, if I was, whether I could come back to the prison. I said I did not know whether I should, but, if I could, I would come up after chapel. You asked me to bring you a clean shirt and some shoes.'

Gould: 'Do you remember advising me to make a further sworn statement?'

Otway: 'I did not advise you to make a further statement to try and get out of your situation. I never mentioned anything about it. I do not remember telling you anything in the presence of the principal turnkey at Coldbath Fields Prison. You sent for me there one night and, when I got to the prison, you said you had made up your mind to tell all you knew about the affair. To the best of my recollection, my reply was, 'I am very glad of it.' I do not believe I made any other observation. I cannot tell under what conditions you made the statement, you had made it to the turnkey before I got there. I did not tell you, in the presence of the turnkey, that by making a statement, you would be entitled to the whole reward and be perfectly in the clear. You were very anxious for me to take Jarvis into custody, but I wanted to hear a little more about it before I took him. I came back the next day and you said there were several other things connected with the case which you would write down for me.'

After the case for the prosecution concluded, Gould rose to his feet, arranged his papers before him, like a qualified advocate, and began his closing statement.

'My Lord, as this is a very intricate case, I am totally unable to explain the nature of the evidence myself. I most earnestly crave your Lordship's protection, as I am undefended.'

'There are some portions of the evidence which, I think, perhaps it is necessary that I should make some remarks upon, although I am not aware that I am compelled to explain every little thing that might transpire. It appears, gentlemen, that although there has been a great mass of evidence produced against me, very little of it actually appears to affect me. I shall explain, in the best manner I can, to you, those parts I think do affect me.'

'Firstly, the witnesses state that I was in the skittle-ground and had no money but three halfpence. Now, gentlemen, the very name of a skittle-ground will convince you of the motive of my denying my pocket there. It is not unlikely, if I had a few shillings of my hard earnings and savings in my pocket, that I should go and throw it away among a parcel of men in a skittle-ground, especially when I could get as much beer as I liked by saying I had no money.'

'One witness has stated that I sent him for a rushlight. I did so, I acknowledge, but I made no secret of it. If I had wanted a rushlight for any particular occasion, I should have gone and got it myself, the shop is but a few yards from the public-house. I sent for it in the open tap-room and he brought it to me in the tap-room.'

'Then, as to the time at which I am stated to have gone home at that night, I would ask you whether it is likely that, on a bright moonlit night, they could tell what time I went in? In their own evidence, they state it was as light as day, yet still, they take it upon themselves to swear it was two o'clock.'

'Regarding my telling the Allens that I had no money, my reason for that must be obvious to you. I owed them between £1 and £2 and there was still something outstanding for boots. If I had told them I had money in my pocket, or that I had been and bought new boots, Allen, being a shoemaker, would naturally have thought it very unprincipled of me to go and lay out my ready money at another shop, while I owed him money.'

'There is a parcel of witnesses who have given various accounts of conversations they say took place between us prior to the murder, but you will have seen with what caution they have managed it so that there should never be a third person to hear those conversations. First, notice Mr Wright. He can recollect everything I said to him, but he does not recollect anything that was said in the presence of Squires. It appears Mr Wright knew all the various places as well as I did. He knew Allen's cottage and he knew the wash-house, the water-closet and the garden, yet he states he never saw a lantern.

'The reason why Squires has been kept out of the way is a mystery to me, but he is not forthcoming today to certify the truth of what Wright has stated.'

'Next, we come to Mr Jobson and Mr Rogers. I will ask you whether their characters are worthy of the least attention. You must have been convinced, by the way in which they answered those questions I put to them, that they are not to be credited for a moment.'

'There is one thing I would particularly wish to draw your attention to, and that is the very unfair, if not illegal, means by which I have been drawn into the predicament in which I now stand. This Sergeant Otway, although he comes here and denies it, knew I was at the Compter, but he would not come to see me there. No, he awaits his opportunity, when he well knew I should be among strangers and should wish not to be known. Mark the time at which he comes, at eleven o'clock at night, when I am in bed and asleep, taking me by surprise, obviously thinking, that day being the first I had been at liberty for some time, that I should have been drinking a little and that would be the best time to get me.'

'When he came to me, he represented himself as a gentleman, sent to me by the Secretary of State, with a special message to offer me £200 if I could give him any information leading to the conviction of the parties concerned in the murder of Mr Templeman. What did I tell him? I at once told him I did not know anything about it and I would have nothing to do with it. He has confessed, here today, that I told him so more than once. I said I would have nothing to do with it for £200. He then sat down and began reasoning with me, telling me that as I was a young man and about to leave the country, how serviceable the money would be to me. He told me how much better it would be to go out with £200 in my pocket than nothing at all and, as I had seen a great deal of trouble, I should be very foolish if I did not now make something out of it if I could.'

'Well, with these persuasions, and the fact that he positively assured me I could not be tried again, I am free to acknowledge I did feel inclined, if I could make anything of it, to do so. I made up my mind to tell a lie, for the sake of the reward. Now, I will ask you, gentlemen, if that was a fair way of transacting business. He then got me to agree to his proposal. After I had said, several times, that I would not have anything to do with it for £200, I said, 'In the event of there not being a conviction, how should I be situated, for, if I was to stop behind, I should lose my passage and lose everything.' He then said, 'Putting that to one side, will you, or would you, if I was to bring you £100 and lay it on this table, tell me who the actual parties were?' I said I would and he then left me.'

'I will ask you, gentlemen, whether you think the conversation, which he states was all that transpired, would occupy half-an-hour. He was obliged to acknowledge he was there for at least half-an-hour. I saw nothing of him again until the next morning, when he came down and, instead of bringing the £100 he had talked about, he brought a warrant.'

'Of course, I found I had been very much taken in, but I did not take any notice of it then. During our journey to London, I asked him how it was I could be apprehended on the warrant. He told me how things stood, that I could be tried for the robbery and, as I had acknowledged to him I knew who the parties were, I could be punished if I did not make a disclosure. I then saw, for the first time, I had been completely taken in and how awkwardly I was situated. He then took me to the station-house and from thence to Bow Street, where I was charged with the robbery. After I had been so charged, he came to me in the lock-up place and told the only way for me to get out of the scrape, was to make a full statement of the whole affair. Then, I should be not only entitled to £100, but to £200. Of course, I could not make any statement at all, but I told him I would consider it and, if he came to me next day at the prison, I would give him a decisive answer. He then left me there, locked up by myself.'

'Finding they had backed me into a corner, and not knowing in what way at all to get out of it, I was driven almost to desperation. I then made up my mind to make it appear that I really had been concerned in the robbery and to accuse innocent parties, with the intent of getting out of it myself. You will think that was a very rash way of proceeding, and so I will allow. I felt it had been rash when I came a little to myself, but I never thought of there being a conviction at that time. It was because he'd promised me I would be able to give evidence, it was on that basis that I made the statement.'

'After I had made up my mind to do so, I sent for him. He came to me in prison and, in the presence of the principal turnkey, I told him I was making this statement, on the condition I was to be, myself, perfectly in the clear. He said he would tell me then, as he had told me before, that I should be admitted as evidence and that I should have the reward.'

'For what reason the principal turnkey has been kept away, I am not aware. He was a witness that would have been very necessary to have been here, to prove that part of my statement, but he is not. I had commenced making this statement to the principal turnkey when the officer came, but I had told him what my motives were for making it and likewise told him I would send for the officer. They thought I was to be admitted as evidence and, on that account, I was not treated as prisoners generally are. I was allowed sheets and tobacco and to buy what I liked. Sergeant Otway also gave me some money there and told me I could have whatever I wanted.'

'Now, gentlemen, I will appeal to you, if this is not an unlawful proceeding, is it not, at least, a very unfair one?'

'Regarding the lantern, it must be very evident to you that I did not know it was there. The reason for my mentioning the lantern, was because there had been a lantern mentioned on a previous occasion. Is it likely that if I'd known there was a lantern in Allen's house, I should have been running anywhere else inquiring after one, as some of the witnesses have tried to make it appear that I was?'

'If I had really been engaged in this horrid affair, should there not be some convincing proof of it? Do you think a transaction of that kind could be carried on, a crime of that kind committed, without something having been traced to the parties themselves? What proof is there about that lantern? None. Where has it been for two years? Whose hands has it been in? If the witnesses were to speak the truth, they do not know whether they left it in the garden or brought it indoors. If they did place it in the cupboard, as they state, a child might have taken it out. Their own children are in the habit of carrying things out and losing them.'

'It would be useless for me to comment any further upon the evidence, as I am sure his Lordship will explain it to you in a much clearer manner than I can.'

Baron Parke duly summed up the facts of the case and after advising the jury of the options available to them, he asked them to retire to consider their verdict. It seems that Gould's closing statement had fallen on deaf ears, as the jury took less than fifteen minutes to return with a 'guilty' verdict.

Baron Parke was not for hanging about either, and he directed Gould be immediately brought forward for sentencing. 'The charge against you has been made out to the satisfaction of the jury, in the justice and propriety of whose verdict both the Lord Chief Justice and I entirely agree.'

'You have been found guilty of the charge laid in the indictment,' Parke continued, 'which was that of burglary, but if your conscience is not already too calloused and hardened, it must be carrying the guilt of a far greater and deeper crime. There can be little doubt in the minds of all who have witnessed this trial, that you are the person by whom the murder of John Templeman was perpetrated.'

'You, yourself, have acknowledged, in the course of your defence, that you were ready to sacrifice an innocent man for the purpose of obtaining a £200 reward. Under all the circumstances, I feel I should be wanting in the duty I owe to the public, filling the post I do, if I did not pass upon you the severest sentence, short of death, that the law will allow me to pronounce,' Parke said, somewhat ominously for Gould.

'That sentence will be transportation for life. I am authorised to add to this a still heavier punishment, which shall be, that you will be sent to a penal colony, to pass the remainder of your existence in hopeless slavery, poverty and misery of the worst description.'

The bleak sentence seemed to find favour among the gallery and a spontaneous round of applause broke out. Gould showed no emotion as he was led from the dock.

10 CHAPTER TEN

On 8 July 1840, Richard Gould set sail for New South Wales, with a party of around 300 fellow convicts, to begin his new life of hopeless slavery, poverty and misery. He would have a long time to reflect on how close he'd been to evading justice and how different the remainder of his life may have been, if he had not been lured from the passenger ship, 'The Elizabeth', by Sergeant Otway's offer of a reward.

Initial newspaper reports claimed Sergeant Otway had been awarded £100, from the £200 reward that had been on offer. This was quickly refuted by the authorities and the following correspondence was leaked to the press:-

'From J.C&C Solicitors to the Lords of Her Majesty's Treasury, 1 August 1840.

In the matter of Richard Gould, formerly known as Arthur Nicholson, a convict under sentence of transportation for life, the memorial of J.C&C humbly showeth:-

That, in the month of May last, your memorialist received private information relative to the supposed knowledge of the above-named convict, of the actual murderer of the late Mr John Templeman, at Islington, of which charge he had been acquitted. The convict was, at that time, a voluntary inmate at the Giltspur Street Compter, preparatory to his taking a free passage to Australia.

That, your memorialist gave information to the Secretary of State for the Home Department, intimating he was in a condition, as he conceived, to make certain disclosures that would probably tend to forward the ends of public justice.

That, on the same evening, your memorialist received a letter from Scotland Yard, citing him to appear there the following morning and make his communication to the Commissioner of Police, to whom the matter had been referred by the Home Department.

That, obedient to that mandate, your memorialist was honoured with a long interview with Colonel Rowan, when he laid before that gentleman a written detail of all the facts that had come to his knowledge. He also penned down such suggestions as occurred to him, relative to the way the matter should proceed, with your memorialist being, at the time, well aware of the peculiarities of temper and the strong prejudices that were imbibed by the convict against a certain class of persons.

That, your memorialist (among other things) urged the necessity of luring Gould, by the offer of a reward and a free pardon to any person who would disclose the name of the actual murderer, so that he might be brought to conviction. Your memorialist, at that time, verily believed Gould was able and felt an inclination to do such a thing.

That, Colonel Rowan was pleased to express his appreciation of the information given and the suggestions made by your memorialist and who signified he would lay the same before the proper authorities.

That, on the second day after that interview, your memorialist was honoured by the receipt of a letter from Colonel Rowan, for the purpose of information being conveyed to Gould, that a reward of £200 would appear in 'The Gazette' on the following evening, upon the conditions that are known to your Lordships.

That, on the receipt of such letter, your memorialist proceeded straightaway to the Compter, to communicate its contents, when, to his great surprise, he found Gould had left the prison earlier that day and was on a vessel lying off Gravesend, in which he was to sail immediately, as a free passenger, to Australia.

That, your memorialist lost no time in making this sudden migration known to the proper authorities, the resulting consequence of which was the capture of Gould, who at such time stood in the character of an emigrant.

That, your memorialist considers he was the primary cause of the re-capture and subsequent conviction of Gould for an offence secondary to the crime of murder. Your memorialist ventures to hazard a conjecture, founded upon the broad basis of public opinion, that the actual murderer has been sentenced to a condign punishment, although not a capital punishment, by which the demands of Justice are fully satisfied.

That, your memorialist, with due humility and respect, submits to your Lordships that he deserves consideration for the part he took in the matter and for the time he expended, as well as some incidental expenses he incurred pending the Inquiry. He, therefore, prays for such recompense as your Lordships, in the plenitude of your power and wisdom, may deem appropriate.

Finally, my Lords, your memorialist begs to represent that, pending the negotiation, he observed the most rigid secrecy and communicated with no person except Colonel Rowan, who can verify the facts herein stated.'

The reply followed on 24 August 1840:-
'From Whitehall to J.C&C
Sir,
The Marquis of Normanby, having transmitted to the Lords of the Treasury your petition, which was placed in his hands by the Commissioner of Police, praying for a portion of the reward offered by Government in the case of the murder of Mr John Templeman, I am directed by his Lordship to inform you that, as the reward was offered 'on conviction of the murderer', the Lords of the Treasury are unable to entertain your application, the murderer not having been convicted.
I am, Sir, your obedient servant.
S.M. Phillips'

Considering the unorthodox and controversial nature of the methods he had employed in bringing Gould to justice, the career of Sergeant Otway was set to stall for a while, but, on the basis that you can't keep a good man down, Otway's career would eventually get back on track and he would go on to become Superintendent of the Metropolitan Police C-Division, before retiring in 1853.

OTHER BOOKS BY THE AUTHOR

True Crimes That Shaped Scotland Yard
True Crimes: Ladykillers
The Curious Case of Charlie Peace
Edinburgh: A Capital City

Printed in Great Britain
by Amazon